ALIGNING
with
HEAVEN

DESTINY IMAGE BOOKS BY DAVID HERZOG

Ancient Portals of Heaven

Glory Invasion

Mysteries of the Glory Unveiled

Mysteries of the Glory Unveiled Study Guide

ALIGNING
with
HEAVEN

Unleashing Ancient Secrets
to Power, Blessing, and Harvest

Dr. David Herzog

DESTINY IMAGE® PUBLISHERS, INC.

P.O. Box 310, Shippensburg, PA 17257-0310

"Promoting Inspired Lives."

Previously published as *Ancient Portals of Heaven* by Destiny Image Publishers
ISBN HC: 978-0-7684-1293-2
Previous ISBN: 978-0-7684-2665-6

This book and all other Destiny Image and Destiny Image Fiction books are available at Christian bookstores and distributors worldwide.

Cover and interior design by Terry Clifton

For more information on foreign distributors, call 717-532-3040.

Reach us on the Internet: www.destinyimage.com.

ISBN 13 TP: 978-0-7684-0743-3

ISBN 13 eBook: 978-0-7684-0744-0

For Worldwide Distribution, Printed in the U.S.A.

1 2 3 4 5 6 7 8 / 19 18 17 16 15

DEDICATION

I would like to dedicate this book first and foremost to the God of Israel who allowed me to receive many of the insights and revelations contained in this book. To my wife, Stephanie, who is the love of my life as well as my best friend and favorite woman speaker and author. I look forward to rediscovering with you all the ancient pathways and spending eternity with you!

To our three girls, who are our greatest joy, Tiffany, Shannon, and Destiny. May you continue to do greater exploits in God than we could have ever imagined.

To Sid Roth, who has pioneered the realm of ministry to the Jew first and to the nations of the world. We thank you for your refreshing friendship, revelation and wisdom, humility and partnership in spreading the gospel to the four corners of the earth.

To Mahesh and Bonnie Chavda for their great love and friendship, wisdom and intercession, and for simply cheering us on these past years.

To all our friends in ministry who are pioneering new realms of glory, revival, and harvest from Jerusalem to the ends of the earth.

Last, but not least, to all our partners and intercessors with whom we credit the amazing favor, harvest of souls, and miracles we have experienced since we first launched out.

CONTENTS

Foreword 11

Introduction 13

Chapter 1   Opening the Ancient Pathways 15

Chapter 2   Ancient Wisdom of Solomon. 29

Chapter 3   A Revival of Wisdom 53

Chapter 4   Ancient Geographical Portals 85

Chapter 5   Seasonal Portals. 99

Chapter 6   Heaven's Glory. 121

Chapter 7   The Courts of Heaven 129

Chapter 8   Ancient Resurrections 141

Chapter 9   Elisha's Double Portion 161

Chapter 10   Ancient Secrets to Worldwide Harvest . . . 175

Chapter 11   The Ishmael-Muslim Connection 187

Chapter 12   The Rise and Fall of Nations. 197

Endnotes 215

FOREWORD

Heaven is drawing closer to earth. This alone will speed up the fulfillment of God's promises—promises for salvation, for restoration of family, finances, and health. But those who learn to move in God's glory will begin to see an acceleration beyond belief. Prayers that you have prayed for years will be answered in minutes. The favor of God increases even more when you bless the apple of His eye—Israel.

Few Christians understand God's heart for Israel and the Jewish people. Both the Old Testament and the New Testament inform us that judgment or blessing is triggered by blessing or cursing Israel. Genesis 12:3 is still in effect. God promises to bless those who bless the Jewish people and curse those who curse them.

But the greater promise is found in Psalm 122:6: *"Pray for the peace of Jerusalem. 'May they prosper who love you.'"* The Hebrew word *prosper* means something greater than money. It means something money cannot purchase. It means "heart peace." As this world races toward self-destruction, those who know their God will be victorious.

I have studied many spiritual laws, but the law of evangelism summarized in Romans 1:16—"*for the Jew first*"—is one of the least-studied and most spiritually rewarding. Over the past three decades, I have traveled the nations to evangelize. Because I always went to the Jew first, a greater door to reach the Gentiles always opened up.

Get ready to explore these ancient pathways that will open rivers in the desert. Doing so will make the invisible realm more real than it has ever been before.

My friend, David Herzog, has removed the veil of mystery from the dynamic tandem of God's glory and Israel. His new book will make you feel like you are born again, again!

SID ROTH
Host, *It's Supernatural!* television program

INTRODUCTION

There are ancient paths and wisdom of the ages that God is restoring in our generation as the Bible says to *"stand in the ways and see, and ask for the old paths, where the good way is, and walk in it; then you will find rest for your souls"* (Jer. 6:16).

As we begin to seek God in these exciting and earthshaking times, God is releasing revelation to recover many ancient secrets and wisdom of times past. These ancient paths allowed Paul and the disciples to access the key to world evangelism in a very short span of time.

Moses received and walked in the ancient paths; he moved in signs, wonders, and miracles that to this day have often been unmatched—at his word the sea parted, all Israel was healed, and an entire generation was set free.

Elijah possessed ancient keys to the spiritual pathways that allowed him to be transported from one location to another, to raise the dead, to command rain to fall on a nation, and to baffle world rulers and entire armies.

Solomon, the wisest man ever to have lived, tapped into ancient pathways that led to peace and stability during his entire reign for Israel and the world. He ruled with great prosperity and justice, and his peaceful reign allowed Israel to develop their military force and travel the world's maritime trade routes. This wisdom also allowed Solomon to experience the glory cloud of God firsthand by aligning himself with the keys and blueprints of Heaven as the glory touched earth.

God has ancient wisdom that has been lost that He wants to release to people in these days. As God promised in the Book of Daniel, knowledge upon the earth will increase upon the earth in the latter days, and so will God's supernatural knowledge and wisdom, enabling us to tap into the fullness of God (see Dan. 12:4).

There are seasonal and geographical portals that once entered into will release phenomenal blessings from an open Heaven that the ancient men of God knew thousands of years ago. Nations will rise and fall in these days based on the wisdom and revelation released in God's Word because the principles that applied to the nations in ancient times also apply today.

As we also align ourselves with not only the God of Israel but the people and land of Israel, we will see the blessings, wisdom, and favor of Abraham, Isaac, Jacob, and the Messiah passed down to us as well, resulting in mass harvest and revival, the wealth of the nations for world evangelism, and the unlocking of Heaven on earth wherever we are.

Chapter 1

OPENING THE ANCIENT PATHWAYS

Thus says the Lord: "Stand in the ways and
see, and ask for the old paths, where the
good way is, and walk in it; then you will
find rest for your souls..." (JEREMIAH 6:16).

There are ancient paths that open up ancient portals into the fullness of the supernatural and the glory of God. Great men of old like Enoch, Moses, Elijah, Adam, Paul, Jesus, and others walked in these ancient paths.

What did these Jewish prophets and apostles know then that may have been lost? What revelation of the ancient paths did they have that. allowed them such communion with God that they could call down fire from Heaven, command rain or shut up the sky, negotiate with God to not destroy a nation, be transported across the earth seemingly at will, make kings and kingdoms tremble at the word of the Lord, be taken up to Heaven without ever tasting death, ignite the evangelism of the known world with just 12 men, and much, much more?

There is a parallel world of the supernatural living side by side this natural realm. Once we tap into the supernatural realm and the revelation of these ancient paths, we will realize it was there all along within our reach. It is just a hand's length away as you reach out for it: *"The kingdom of heaven is at hand,"* Jesus said (Matt. 4:17).

These truths have been embedded in the Word of God but are not always apparent to the casual observer. In the Book of Malachi, God leaves us a key that was to be perpetuated. There was no real prophet or direct communication with Heaven that is recorded from the last book in the Hebrew Scriptures until the Gospels of Mathew, Mark, Luke, and John, and the appearance of Jesus.

Imagine you are on a space shuttle in outer space, and you get a message from the Houston Control Center: "We are not going to have any communication for quite a long time, maybe years, so listen carefully. These are your last instructions before we resume communication." If that were me, I would be intently listening to those last instructions to carry me through.

Let's see what the last few verses of the Book of Malachi contain—written hundreds of years before the Book of Matthew:

> *Remember the Law of Moses, My servant, which I*
> *commanded him in Horeb for all Israel, with the*
> *statutes and judgments. Behold, I will send you*
> *Elijah the prophet before the coming of the great*

*and dreadful day of the Lord. And He will turn
the hearts of the fathers to the children, and the
hearts of the children to their fathers, lest I come
and strike the earth with a curse* (Malachi 4:4-6).

God is talking about the mantles of Moses and Elijah. The
fact that Moses and Elijah appear again in the New Testament on the Mount of Transfiguration and again in Revelation
point to something God is clearly trying to get across (see Matt.
17:1-11; Rev. 11:1-14). Moses carried the laws and ordinances of
God—which were the beginning of restoring the ancient pathways back to God—and the supernatural, which God says not
to forget as we enter into the New Testament. Along with these
keys would be the power and mantle of Elijah.

Moses and Elijah were powerful types of how God wants
to continue to operate in His people. Moses received the Ten
Commandments, which are still the foundational laws and
ancient paths that lead to the beginning of walking with God
for a person, city, or nation. Loving God with all your heart,
mind, soul, and strength, and loving your neighbor as yourself
are one of the first ancient paths. All the other laws are based
on the first two.

Once these laws are removed, entire civilizations can self-
destruct. With God's power Moses confronted and shook the
most powerful kingdoms and authorities, including Pharaoh
and the magicians of Egypt, with signs and wonders following (see Exod. 7-11). He saw the Red Sea split, an entire nation
healed, miracles of supernatural provision, entire armies
destroyed, and he led his people to the verge of the promised
land (see Exod. 14:13-21; Num. 21; Exod. 16; Num. 21:21-35;

Deut. 32:48-52). Jesus also mentions Moses, and Moses and Elijah both appeared to Jesus as well.

Elijah was not just a prophet but also moved in the most unusual miracles and signs for that time. He also would be able to be transported from one physical location to another (see 1 Kings 18:7-12). He could command the rain to stop for three and a half years or to start again (see 1 Kings 17:1; 1 Kings 18:1). He raised the dead and did provisional miracles, like multiplying the widow's oil (see 1 Kings 17:17-24; 1 Kings 17:9-16). Both Elijah and his servant Elisha, who continued in the same mantle, confronted the power of their day, Jezebel (see 1 Kings 19; 2 Kings 9). The fact that Elijah raised up another to walk in his mantle is also a type that God wanted to highlight and continue through Jesus.

Jesus, the Messiah, demonstrated attributes similar to those of Moses and Elijah. Jesus said in John 5:46-47, *"If you believed Moses, you would believe Me; for he wrote about Me. But if you do not believe his writings, how will you believe My words?"*

Moses and Elijah had received and tapped into the ancient paths that opened up entire nations to God and His power and love. Jesus came at a time when the ancient paths were lost. The power of the Hebrew Scriptures and the Ten Commandments were available, but the revelation was lost on how to tap back into that supernatural world while living on the earth. As Jesus said in John 5:46, *"If you believed Moses, you would believe Me."*

He did not come to abolish the law and the prophets, but to fulfill them (see Matt. 5:17). In other words, Jesus did not say that now we are free under grace to break all Ten

Commandments. Only that we are not saved by observing the law but by His shed blood on the cross.

He demonstrated how God's Word should be lived out—not in a religious spirit, but in a supernatural way. When you think about it, the only book that they had at the time of Jesus was the Old Testament, as Jesus read from Isaiah and said that the Word was fulfilled in their hearing. It actually was never called the Old Testament but simply the Scriptures or the Word of God. When Paul told Timothy to study to show himself approved, the only Bible they had at the time was what we now call the Old Testament. Peter preached from the book of Joel to explain the outpouring of the Holy Spirit that came on the biblical feast of Pentecost. What Jesus did was to take them out of dead rituals, as He now became the reason for the season and the fulfillment of the laws of God. He now was the Word that became flesh, taking the Word of God—otherwise known as the laws and principles of God—from dead ritual to supernatural power.

For example, most believers today would agree that the laws of God in the Ten Commandments are still applicable today, as they are used in many courthouses and used to be in the public schools as a foundation for governing a society and thus creating our Judeo-Christian heritage. The only difference is that the laws do not save us, nor do we rely on them as our means to salvation apart from Christ. It is only by grace through faith in the shed blood of Jesus are we saved.

That does not mean that we should not still abide by the commands of God which were given as a way for humankind to live upon the earth. Praise God that today we are not under the yoke of trying to fulfill the law to be saved. Yet those laws are still applicable for daily living—do not steal, do not kill, do not covet, laws of sowing and reaping, laws of gravity, speeding laws, laws of rest, etc. To function and operate at full capacity while on the earth without curses but with blessing, these laws were written for our benefit. The entire Word of God is still valid today, both old and new. The principles have not changed, only the application. God has always required blood sacrifice, though today it's Jesus's blood that covers our sins, but the requirement for blood to be cleansed has never changed.

For example, one of the first ancient paths occurred through blood sacrifice. This opened up humans to God, and recovered what was lost in the Garden of Eden. God required blood as a sacrifice to reconnect people to God (see Heb. 13:12). Jesus did not do away with this law of God but became the sacrifice so that we could all go boldly to the throne (see Heb. 4:16). Even when blood sacrifice is done in the demonic realms, it opens up demonic supernatural power for evil. It is a doorway to the supernatural, whether for good or evil.

Before Jesus came on the scene, God required blood sacrifices. The glory of God appeared in Solomon's temple after the blood sacrifices and opened a realm of the supernatural that Adam and Eve had lost. From the time of Adam onward, sacrifice was always a blood sacrifice. Today, God still requires blood, but the good news of the gospel is that He paid for it with His blood for us! When we rediscover the power of the blood of the Passover Lamb that was slain—Jesus—we tap into the supernatural. Even during communion, when the revelation of the blood is revealed, we have seen many instantly healed and delivered and the glory of God begin to totally invade the room. God still responds to the revelation of the blood of Jesus that needs to be revisited by believers today, who have lost the revelation of the blood.

Basically, all the portals and ancient paths have been copied by the enemy and used to open up demonic pathways into evil portals that allow the enemy to do similar things. But God's power is superior. While the magicians of Egypt could do the same miracles as Moses for a little while, they could not match the power of God that shook Egypt (see Exod. 8:7,18). Moses had received and walked in the ancient paths that even caused the laws of nature to be changed.

When Moses discovered that he was a Hebrew and belonged to the God of Israel, not to pagan Egypt, he began to reconnect to and pray to the God of Israel and identify himself with the people of God. This new sense and understanding of his identity began his journey into the supernatural as God began to reveal the ancient paths. One of these was the command to put the blood on the doorposts of each house—this would protect Israel from the last plague. He was given the lost keys and access into the protection and power of God that Israel had lost and forgotten as slaves. Once God began revealing these ancient paths to Moses, Pharaoh's demonic sorcerers were no match for the power of God.

Why did people think that Jesus was one of the prophets of the Old Testament that had come back to life? Jesus walked in such power that His contemporaries could only imagine that He was, in fact, one of the prophets of old or even John the Baptist.

> *When Jesus came into the region of Caesarea Philippi, He asked His disciples, saying, "Who do men say that I, the Son of Man, am?" So they*

said, "Some say John the Baptist, some Elijah, and others Jeremiah or one of the prophets" (Matthew 16:13-14).

The people were trying to please God with the Scriptures, but they needed a shepherd who could show them the way back to the ancient paths through a fresh revelation of the written Word. Since the time of the prophets of old, Israel had not had any leaders who could connect them to the God of Heaven in a supernatural way as Moses, Elijah, and the great patriarchs had. Jesus performed miracles similar to those of the prophets—miracles of power, provision, healing, deliverance, and resurrection—and He told them to believe Him by the miracles He performed.

Enoch walked so close to God that he disappeared from the face of the earth (see Gen. 5:24). Elijah left the earth in a similar way without tasting death. I believe that once these ancient paths are opened, some will have fully tapped in and will never taste death, as it was intended in the beginning before humans fell.

How did Elijah transport from one place to another? How did he tap into the supernatural realm where physical limitations disappear? Just as there are flight paths for air travel that, if followed, allow the plane to travel back and forth from one country to another, so there are supernatural grid lines in the spirit that, if followed, allow one to travel from one dimension or location to another.

I have heard people's testimonies of going through a tunnel or road up to a bright light into Heaven, only to be sent back because it was not their time to die. The same goes for those who were briefly taken to hell along a dark path or trail, but then cried out to Jesus and were saved after their near-death experience, then coming back to tell about it. Also, we have heard of those who were formerly involved in witchcraft talk about how their spirit and at times their bodies traveled back and forth along demonic power lines. The same holds true for those who see portals open up, as Jacob did, with angels ascending and descending. Other Scriptures speak about a doorway and windows opening into the heavens, allowing a certain access that otherwise would not be there had those portals, doors, or pathways not been opened.

Remember, the spiritual and natural worlds work in parallel. The natural world was modeled after the supernatural. Adam and Eve were able to walk in both the natural and supernatural as they walked in the Garden, but they also walked with God Himself. The grid seems to work in such a way that it moves up and down and to and fro. Jacob saw the grid open up, allowing angels to ascend to and descend from Heaven. There are also demonic gateways and grids that satan copied from Heaven that he uses along with his followers.

> *Now there was a day when the sons of God came to present themselves before the Lord, and Satan came also among them. And the Lord said to Satan, "From where do you come?" So Satan answered the Lord and said, "From going to and fro on the earth, and from walking back and forth on it"* (Job 1:6-7).

Satan was able to travel across the earth and also from earth to Heaven illegally along these demonic grids. That is how those involved in the occult, astral projection, and many forms of witchcraft are able to travel out of their bodies from one place to another.

God said through Amos, *"Though they dig into hell, from there My hand shall take them; though they climb up to heaven, from there I will bring them down"* (Amos 9:2). Here we see the up and down pattern again in this grid.

The deception of the occult is that one can be offered the supernatural realms without first turning to God through His Son Jesus. The way back to the ancient paths is through the front door, not the back door. The Bible says, *"salvation is of the Jews"* (John 4:22). The Jewish Messiah, Jesus (*Yeshua* in Hebrew), came to restore what the Jewish forefather of the faith and the church had once received.

Once a mantle is acquired upon the earth it only needs to be awakened again and received by a person or people to reactivate its power. Today the mantle of John G. Lake's healing rooms has been picked up, and now healing rooms are not only occurring at the same location they once were, in Spokane, Washington, but in churches nationwide. Others today such as Benny Hinn appear to have picked up a mantle similar to Kathryn Khulman. I believe it is possible to ask God for a mantle that someone gone before you has received, because the last generation always raises the bar for the next to start out on a higher level.

Elisha valued and asked for even double of what Elijah carried, and he received his mantle. Once Elisha learned the ancient pathways from Elijah, he was able to fully operate in it and see even greater works than Elijah. Jesus, the Jewish Messiah for the entire world, came and became that doorway back into the good and ancient paths. Any other doorways leading to these realms are not of God but are deception from the evil one. Jesus is the portal, door, and pathway that connects us back to the ancient paths.

> *Then Jesus said to them again, "Most assuredly, I say to you, I am the door of the sheep. All who ever came before Me are thieves and robbers, but the sheep did not hear them. I am the door. If anyone enters by Me, he will be saved, and will go in and out and find pasture"* (John 10:7-9).

Jesus is the pathway to enter back into the ancient ways and tap into what the ancients knew and more. Since Abraham, God has chosen the Jewish people to steward the keys and oracles of the Word of God, and from them would come the Jewish Messiah, Savior of the world. God showed the Jewish prophets keys and patterns that open up the heavens on the earth. When we connect to these ancient pathways and patterns, we too will see the glory of God unleashed in ways that may have never occurred before. That is why it says that *"salvation is of the Jews"* (John 4:22).

The 12 Jewish apostles became carriers of the glory that has spread to the entire known world today. The Hebrew Scriptures were available, but Jesus brought back the revelation of how to activate the ancient pathways, allowing the church to once again experience what Moses, Elijah, and many other ancient prophets knew. It is like the movie *Raiders of the Lost Ark*, where an archaeologist discovers a hidden map disclosing the location of the ark of the covenant. As he follows the patterns and instructions of the map, the ark's power reawakens after thousands of years of waiting for someone with the revelation to rediscover it.

I recently ministered to a psychic at a health food store in my hometown of Sedona. The lady behind the counter began to tell me how she levitated that week off the floor in her room when she invited 10,000 Buddhas to enter into her. I asked her how high she got—to which she told me a few feet. I shocked her when I replied, "Is that all?" And I began to explain to her how what she was experiencing was so inferior to God's power through Jesus, the true, pure, undefiled source. She began to tell me that she once died in a hospital bed and that Jesus appeared to her; she came back to life and greatly respects and loves Jesus. I asked her how she felt when she levitated. She told me that she did not feel right and that she felt there was something negative about it all. She told me that in the middle of this experience, Jesus appeared to her and took her to the outside of the Kingdom of Heaven, but for some reason she could not enter inside. Then a great light shone, and a voice came out of it that said, *"No man comes to the Father but through Me"* (see John 14:6).

I explained to her that the only way to experience God, the Creator of all life and power, was through His Son Jesus, and that Jesus was the doorway into knowing God, Heaven, and all that is pure. Any other way, though it may have some power, is a polluted well that leads to spiritual death. I also shared with her that God is a jealous God and that He says He is the only doorway. Other pathways may have some kind of power, but He is the only way to eternal life and to knowing the true source of all love and power. She began to weep and asked to know more about this pathway, Jesus

God showed her the most beautiful place, the Kingdom of Heaven, from the outside looking in, but He also showed her that she could not get in through illegal channels—only through the main door, not a back door or demonic door. Jesus was gracious to visit her because she sincerely did not know which path was the right one; she was simply a seeker who was open and ready to hear the truth.

If we as believers don't enter into the supernatural through Jesus, how are we going to lead those in the occult who are already operating in the demonic grids that allow them to travel and channel? If we offer them words without demonstration and an inferior level of the supernatural, why would they want to join us, or adhere to a gospel that is in word only? We can't just say through Jesus there is more power; we have to be living it ourselves to show the difference as Moses did with the magicians and as Elijah did when he challenged the prophets of Baal. Paul said the gospel was not in word only, but in power and demonstration (see 1 Thess. 1:5).

And my speech and my preaching were not with persuasive words of human wisdom, but in demonstration of the Spirit and of power, that your faith should not be in the wisdom of men but in the power of God (1 Corinthians 2:4-5).

Chapter 2

ANCIENT WISDOM
OF SOLOMON

GOD-GIVEN WISDOM

The ancient people of Israel acquired so much wisdom that much of it is only now being rediscovered. When Solomon received the wisdom of God, the entire world was transformed and went into a quantum leap of advancement. This included improvement in human relations, relations with God, wisdom in business, commerce, and finances, and even some inventions of Solomon. First Kings 4:29-31 records,

> *And God gave Solomon exceptionally much wisdom and understanding, and breadth of mind like the sand on the seashore. Solomon's wisdom excelled the wisdom of all the people of the East and all the wisdom of Egypt. For he was wiser than all other men.... His fame was in all the nations round about* (AMP).

Can you imagine that Solomon was wiser than all men on the earth? Also imagine that Solomon was wiser than the combined wisdom of Egypt upon which their empire was built. And he was even wiser than all the wise men of the East who were known for unusual wisdom.

As a result of this God-given wisdom, Solomon excelled in many areas. Besides being the most powerful king in the world, he was a builder, an inventor, an author, a songwriter, and a naturalist who studied all forms of plants, flora, and the entire animal kingdom (see 1 Kings 4:33). It is likely that he brought in exotic animals and plants from around the world to study. Because he was so rich and his kingdom was at peace, he had much free time to explore his insatiable interests, to establish a vast collection of artwork, and to gather the world's best singers and musicians. The public zoo in Israel as well as the museums must have been quite a sight to behold, besides the splendor of the Temple and the king's wisdom.

Israel invented the Bessemer process of refining steel in a large blast furnace complex, which suddenly developed during the time of King Solomon and King David. Such evidence is found in the remains of the smelting facilities at Ezion-Geber (in southern Israel) termed, "the biggest smelting installation in the ancient East...consisting of a regular ultramodern furnace with a system of air channels, chimney flues, and openings for specific purposes." Concerning the excavation of these smelting facilities in ancient Israel, Werner Keller, in his book *The Bible as History*, states the following:

> Remains of an extensive settlement were excavated. The most interesting things were casting-moulds and a vast quantity of copper slag.... In the middle

of a square walled enclosure an extensive building came into view. The green discoloration on the walls left no doubt as to the purpose of the building: it was a blast furnace. The mud-brick walls had two rows of openings.... The whole thing was a proper up-to-date blast furnace, built in accordance with a principle that celebrated its resurrection in modern industry a century ago as the Bessemer system.[1]

Werner Keller also writes the following: "Nowhere else in the Fertile Crescent, neither in Babylonia or Egypt, was such a great furnace to be found.... Ezion-Geber (in southern Israel) was the Pittsburgh of old Palestine."[2]

Experts have dated the ancient blast furnace to "within the period of Solomon's reign, after 1000 B.C." It was most likely used to smelt and process the iron and copper ores into instruments for Solomon's use in building the Temple of God. Because ancient Israel had mastered the Bessemer system, it was likely one of the most industrially-advanced civilizations of the ancient world. With the largest ore smelting capacity, they were able to make goods for trade and more weapons than any other nation.

This is not to mention that Israel under King Solomon was self-sufficient in food, as the Bible records. Even when the Queen of Sheba came to visit, she noticed this. They were a major agricultural society and a major food exporter. They also had a huge land force, which made them unstoppable, and was one of the reasons there were no major wars under King Solomon—no one dared.

King Solomon was not content to be a land power alone, however; he also wanted Israel to become a major maritime force in the world with fleets based in the Red Sea. To accomplish this, King Solomon (and even King David before him) made alliances with Phoenicia, originally known as Tyre and Sidon. His close alliances with the Phoenician city-states produced great naval and maritime fleets that carried news of Solomon's projects and activities wherever they sailed. The alliance was so strong that the Phoenicians sailed with the Israelites in joint ventures as one unit. The Israelite-Phoenician alliance meant that Israel was, along with Phoenicia and Egypt, a dominant military power.[3] First Kings 9:26-27 confirms this when it states,

> *King Solomon also built a fleet of ships at Ezion Geber, which is near Elath on the shore of the Red Sea, in the land of Edom. Then Hiram sent his servants with the fleet, seamen who knew the sea, to work with the servants of Solomon.*

King Hiram was the king of Tyre and Sidon (or what we call today Phoenicia), and Phoenicia was also a friend and ally of King David and King Solomon. The fact that both the Israelites and the Phoenicians had a common language, a common enemy, and a common Semitic race helped to unite them. The Phoenician language was almost identical to Hebrew. Indeed, the languages were so closely related that when Elijah stayed at a Phoenician widow's home in Zarephath, a suburb of Sidon, they had no difficulty communicating (see 1 Kings 17:9-16).

It has long been known that Phoenician ships traded throughout the Mediterranean, the western shores of Europe and Africa, and the British Isles, and it has recently been discovered that the Phoenicians' trade routes extended all over Asia, India, and even to the New World. Phoenicia's main trading partner for food was the area inhabited by Israel, which the Bible also confirms (see Ezek. 27:17).[4] The Israel-Phoenician alliance allowed Israel to be a dominant military power at the time. In fact, when King David began to prepare for Solomon to build the great Temple in Jerusalem, besides the gold and silver he gathered from his conquests in other nations, he also gathered *"bronze and iron beyond measure, for it is so abundant"* (1 Chron. 22:14).

Where could David get the massive amounts of copper ore needed for his artisans to make brass for the Temple that would be "beyond weighing"? David weighed everything else, but not the bronze or the iron. How many millions of talents of bronze and iron would warrant this description? The loot of war victories or payments from other nations for peace would have to have been imported. But such an abundance could not all have come from Israel's surrounding nations that it was beyond measure. Since King David was allied with the Phoenicians, he most likely acquired them from the nations the Phoenicians traded with.

According to the late Dr. Barry Fell, who is a professor of invertebrate zoology and an amateur epigrapher, historical evidence exists to prove that copper trading occurred between North America and the Old World prior to, during, and after the reign of King David. Dr. Fell pointed to inscriptions he identified as Phoenician found in the New World in places such as New Hampshire's "Mystery Hill." If Dr. Fell's claims are to be believed, King David's massive accumulation of copper ore for the Temple that Solomon would build could have come from the Phoenicians' North American trading routes in the Great Lakes area.

Around the northern shore of Lake Superior, and on the adjacent Ile Royale, there are approximately 5,000 ancient copper mine workings. In 1953 and 1956, Professor Roy Drier led two Michigan mining and technology expeditions to the sites. Charcoal found at the bases of the ancient mining pit yielded carbon dates indicating that the mines had been operated between 2000 B.C. and 1000 B.C. The most conservative estimates by mining engineers show that at least 500 million pounds of metallic copper were removed over that span, and that there is no evidence as to *what became of it.*

What is amazing is that 1000 B.C. was right around the time of King David's rule according to the *Encyclopedia Britannica* and *Harper's Bible Dictionary.* Since these dates coincide, I find it likely that King David used this copper in his worldwide search for raw material for the dedication of the Temple. It is noted that the Lake Superior mines were worked to exhaustion exactly at the time when King David was stockpiling copper ore "beyond calculation" for the building of the Temple in Jerusalem. Also the fact that *there is no evidence as to what became of it* can possibly be answered from the Bible.

As mentioned earlier, Israel was the only known nation at the time to have the most advanced and massive copper smelting facility to process the copper ore. And, as such, ancient Israel appears to have been the major copper user at the time— such evidence is found in the remains of smelting facilities at Ezion-Geber in southern Israel.

King David, and Israel in general as well as Solomon in particular, were very likely the biggest importers in the world of copper and many other raw materials that were being collected for the Temple that Solomon eventually built. This was

David's greatest desire, to build God a Temple to be worshiped in as billions went into it, and he acquired so much copper that it was the only precious metal "beyond weighing," as it far exceeded the gold and silver stockpiles that he did weigh. Solomon's building projects went far beyond anything David himself could have imagined, as there had to be great demand in their region and beyond for enough raw materials to build the most magnificent and expensive building on earth to host the God of Heaven.

WHAT BECAME OF IT?

The basic observation of most scholars that have searched for the whereabouts of the copper in Lake Superior is that "there is no evidence as to what became of it."[5] It may have its meaning in Solomon's Temple. Even secular sources have confirmed that North American copper mines ran out of ore around 1000 B.C. Another note is that archaeologists have maintained that there was no Bronze Age in North America. Mineralogists also conclude that the missing metal may have been shipped overseas, as they reason it is impossible for so large a quantity of metal to have vanished through wear and tear. Also, there is the proof of the largest smelting installation in the region located in Israel with large amounts of copper slag found on its walls.

The fact that Phoenicia was allied with Israel, dominated the commerce of the Mediterranean Sea, and sailed into the Atlantic Ocean to reach ports in West Africa and northwest Europe is amazing, but how far into the Atlantic did they sail? Many artifacts of Phoenician origin have confirmed the presence of the Phoenicians in the New World. For instance, shrines dedicated to the Phoenician/Canaanite god Baal have been found in New England and other parts of America with even a large temple observatory site located at what has been known as Mystery Hill in North Salem, New Hampshire, covering twenty acres.[6]

The Phoenicians quickly sent ambassadors to Israel when they heard of King David's death to continue the alliance with Solomon that they had started with David (see 1 Kings 5:1). The fact that King Hiram initiated the action to stay in good relations with Israel also points to the fact that Israel was a greater power than Phoenicia, since the lesser power usually will seek favor with a greater power to protect its interests.

The ancient world was more technologically advanced than we have imagined; inventions that the modern world claims— like the Bessemer process and ships that could travel to the New World—have in actuality only been rediscovered. Just imagine the ramifications of visits to the New World by ancients from the Old World with its maritime trading routes and knowledge of the sea, commerce, and technology, and the knowledge of the glory of the God of Israel.

ANCIENT ISRAELITES IN ANCIENT AMERICA

Consider additional evidence that worshipers of the God of Israel, Yahweh, were present in ancient America. Near Albuquerque, New Mexico, ancient Hebrew inscriptions (called the Los Lunas inscription) record on stone the Exodus 20 version of the Ten Commandments—though a good deal of controversy in the academic community surrounds the stone's antiquity.

Dr. Fell, once a professor emeritus of Harvard University and internationally renowned expert on ancient languages and the founder of the National Epigraphic Society, has noted that "the inscriptions, written in ancient Hebrew letters of the style of the Moab Stone, (also found in the Mideast) about 1000 B.C. were not translated until 1949."[7] No matter what the exact date, it does predate the arrival of Columbus by at least 1,000 years. A more recent date would pose a problem. There were no Hebrew nations in the Old World in the fourth century that existed or could have achieved such a feat.

Apparently some were so alarmed about any evidence of Israelites in ancient America that they tried to pull a hoax to discredit the discovery by placing fake artifacts in the same region during a trial, trying to make the new artifacts look Greek, left behind by a Greek exile. In a 1986 court trial, it was proven and demonstrated by expert epigraphers and linguists that the other Greek "artifacts" were hoaxes made since 1979.[8] The end result of the court trial affirmed the evidence that Israelites were present in ancient America by demonstrating conclusively that the Los Lunas inscriptions are a record of the Ten Commandments in ancient Hebrew.

Again, if Dr. Fell's Los Lunas claims are accurate, 1000 B.C. would place this inscription during the reigns of King David and Solomon, when Israel was united and when it was still serving the God of the Bible. This most likely occurred during King Solomon's reign, because such transoceanic expeditions in the ancient world required the very large financial backing and ample supply of human resources that only the king of a wealthy nation could supply. Even Columbus needed the financial support of the Queen of Spain.

What other Old World nation would fund exploration and mining efforts in the New World, leaving behind classical Hebrew inscriptions of devotion to God around 1000 B.C.?

Kings after Solomon frequently worshiped Baal and other gods and would have left inscriptions to these gods. Since King David was always involved in military battles, it appears that King Solomon with his reign of peace would have had the time and resources for such an expedition—not to mention an unmatched scientific curiosity of the world and a desire to study all manner of fauna and flora from around the world (see 1 Kings 4:29-33; 10:22). David could not have had the energy to expend on world exploration as he was constantly in battles, but Solomon ruled during a time of world peace, at least in his area of the known world. Solomon also had the greatest wealth—the two combinations that could lead to such a feat with his alliances.

Also, ancient American *dolmens* (megalithic monuments consisting of large slab stone positioned atop smaller supporting stones), which parallel Old World dolmens, have been found. Some in modern academia have tried to write it off as glacial "erratics" to avoid the truth and obvious evidence that the Old World had ties to ancient America. They avoid the obvious evidence that we were not the only ones to visit America, and these facts have often been hidden from the American people.[9]

Other evidence of ancient worshipers of the God of Israel in America has been noted on the "Decalogue Tablet," a stone tablet having an ancient Hebrew inscription of the Ten Commandments, unearthed in Ohio in 1860. The tablet not only has an inscription of the Ten Commandments on it, but it also has the depiction of "an individual meant to represent Moses carved in great detail on the front of the tablet and a handle at the bottom of the tablet, which may have been constructed to create a strap."[10]

The tablet was found in a grave with other goods, buried with a body in an earthen mound. A portable tablet with the Ten Commandments in ancient Hebrew found in a grave could very well point to an ancient Levitical priest present with the Israelite explorers in ancient America. Whether or not everyone agrees on the actual date, analysts now confess, after seeing the tablet in ancient Hebrew and many other artifacts found on American soil, that "the time frame of continental exploration is suddenly retreating to 1000 B.C. or earlier."[11]

Other artifacts cited by another epigrapher, Gloria Farley, "made notable findings of ancient inscriptions left by the Libyans, Celts, and Phoenicians who ascended the Mississippi, Arkansas and Cirraron Rivers."[12]

The Ten Commandments having been found in both Ohio and New Mexico, both great distances apart, along with Phoenician artifacts, leads to an unsettling conclusion to our modern western mindset and pride of our achievements: ancient Israelites and other Old World nations explored the New World and were more widespread than originally thought. Modern academia has an almost "mystical" addiction to the false notion that has been believed and pounded into students that nobody could have discovered America before Columbus. Columbus, in 1492, may have only rediscovered the New World.

King Solomon's fleets would return to Israel only after voyages lasting at least three years: *Once every three years the merchant ships came bringing gold, silver, ivory, apes, and monkeys. So King Solomon surpassed **all the kings of the earth in riches and wisdom**"* (1 Kings 10:22-23). A voyage of three years could only mean that it was a fleet devoted to world exploration. That these fleets would return with lots of wildlife, such as apes and peacocks, showed they traveled to many different continents on extended voyages.

Some claim that ancient Jewish graves have been found in America. An ancient inscription from the first century, found on the Bat Creek Stone in Tennessee, was assumed to be Cherokee in origin until it was later identified as paleo-Hebrew and controversially recognized by Hebrew scholars who have studied it as a Hebrew text of the first century.

Dr. Robert Stieglitz reads it as "a comet for the Hebrews," with reference to Halley's Comet, which hung over Jerusalem "like a flaming sword" in the year A.D. 69 during the first revolt. The evidence suggests that Kentucky and Tennessee became havens of refuge for persecuted Hebrews.[13] A member of the Hebrew and Middle Eastern Studies of Harvard University, who identified the Los Lunas inscription found in New Mexico as ancient Hebrew, added that a number of Hebrew inscriptions have been found in American graves that originally were incorrectly identified as Indian.[14]

It was even said that Christopher Columbus, the man credited with "discovering" the New World, proclaimed that these newly discovered "Indians" were in fact of Jewish origins. Columbus even suggested that Spain could "recruit their bodies and their wealth to assist Europeans in a final crusade to crush Islam and reclaim Jerusalem."[15]

Not only that, but on August 3, 1492, due to the Edict of Expulsion, all Jews were required to leave Spain. Boarding their vessels before midnight, and sailing a half hour before sunrise, Columbus and his crew set out on his now-famous voyage as many believe he took Jews with him the same day they were being expelled.

Hebrew astronomers like Abraham Zcuto had consulted seeking a sea route to India around Africa, furnishing the celestial timetables. Also, Rabbi Levi ben Gershon invented a quadrant known as Jacob's Staff. This angle-measuring device was used by the explorers Columbus and Da Gama, and by Ferdinand Magellan, the first person to circumnavigate the earth.

Abraham Ibn Esra, Jacob ben Machir, and Jacob Carsoni developed a technical apparatus like the Astrolabe, used to determine the latitude and longitude of a position. Cartography, the art and science of making maps and charts, was also an area of Jewish expertise in Europe. One such specialist was Abraham Cresques, known as "The Master of Maps and Compasses." Another was his son, Jehudah ben Cresques, who administered several schools of cartography, thus preparing for the "age of discovery" on their horizon. And it was a young mariner and cartographer who was to combine these factors into a radical plan to reach the East by sailing west across the Atlantic Ocean—Christopher Columbus.[16]

There is additional evidence that the Israelites met ancient Native American tribes. One sign of a Hebrew presence in ancient New England is the presence of hundreds of Semitic/Hebrew root words in the languages of the Eastern Algonquin Indians and other tribes. The Cherokee Indians seem to have the most resemblance to the ancient Israelites in their dress (fringes), manner of worship, and other customs that are almost identical to Hebrew customs and worship. They have their own "Day of Atonement," which is very similar to Israel's.

The Northern Cherokee Nation of Old Louisiana Territory has recently shocked the world by claiming that their ancient oral legends tell of a Cherokee migration made to America from the area in Israel known as Masada. This startling evidence is being offered to the public by Beverly Baker Northup, who is the spokesperson for their organization.

The story has been kept alive among the Cherokee people that the *Sicarii,* who escaped from Masada, are some of our ancestors who managed to cross the water to this land, and later became known as Cherokees. In addition to other startling claims, there is also the belief by the Northern Cherokee that a rock that was uncovered in Tennessee in 1889 that is named the Bat Creek Stone proves a transatlantic connection to Jews. Northup believes that the scratched writings on the rock indicate that the stone is evidence of a first-century Atlantic crossing to America by these escaped Jews who later became known as the Northern Cherokee Indians.[17]

For instance, the similarity in marriage customs among many Indian tribes is striking. A widow could not marry without the express permission of her brother-in-law. This custom only existed among the American Indians and the Israelites. Like the Jews, the Indians had their own "Day of Atonement" in which all insults were forgiven and all disputes buried. The Indian totem corresponded in significance with the Israelites' ark of the covenant. The latter was a chest carried on poles that must never touch the ground. In wartime the Israelites carried the ark, and the Indians carried their totem. Among the Israelites, the new moon was linked to the Sabbath, and the festival of the new moon was a biblical feast. Also among the Indians ceremonies of the new moon were of great importance.

According to Dr. Joseph Mahen of Atlanta, Georgia, an expert in ancient Indian ethnology, the Yuchis Indians who migrated to the Oklahoma territory show evidence of contact with the Old World in historic times. They, like the Chero-kees, have a custom unique among American Indians. They are racially and linguistically different from their neighbors. Every year on the 15th day of the sacred month of harvest, in the fall, they make a pilgrimage. For eight days they live in "booths" with roofs open to the sky, covered with branches and leaves and foliage. During this festival they call upon the name of God.

The ancient Israelites had virtually the same custom. In the harvest season in the fall, on the 15th day of the sacred month of harvest (the seventh month), they celebrate the "festival of booths" for eight days. During this time they lived in temporary booths covered with branches, leaves, and fronds. This festival goes back to the time of Moses and the Exodus from ancient Egypt (see Lev. 23). How did two totally separate groups celebrate the same custom?[18]

Dr. Cyrus Gordon, of Brandeis University in Boston, was privileged to sit in on one of the fall harvest festivals of the Yuchi Indians and listened to their chants, songs, and sacred ceremonies. An expert in Hebrew, Minoan, and many Middle Eastern languages, he was incredulous. As he listened, he exclaimed to his companion, "They are speaking the Hebrew names for God!"

THE WISDOM OF THE ANCIENTS

King Solomon's wisdom had caused the entire known world to go into a quantum leap of advancement. In fact, during Solomon's reign, as a result of their alliance with Israel, the technical skills of the Phoenicians increased markedly. International power and influence characterized the Phoenicians from

1000–700 B.C.—the time when the Israelites left the area and the city-states were left alone. After 700 B.C., the term "Phoenicians" describes a people with severely reduced numbers and influence due to the fact that the Israelites had, by then, left the area.

Egypt allied itself with Solomon during his reign; it was, of course, in their best interests to do so since Israel had become a more dominant military presence. Egypt's Pharaoh even offered his daughter to Solomon to secure such an alliance.

Interestingly, however, Egyptian wisdom reached its highest ethical point during this period of alliance. The fact that the Pharaoh of Egypt was also Solomon's father-in-law could explain how much of this wisdom might have easily passed on to Egypt. Dr. Barry Fell writes again,

> Around 1100 B.C., Egyptian wisdom writing reached its highest ethical point, as it counsels against arrogance, snobbery, ill-temper, and oppressing the poor. It stresses courtesy, deference, contentment, tolerance and kindness…[19]

Even the Queen of Sheba from Ethiopia was astonished by Solomon's kingdom. Perhaps she thought the reports were exaggerated until she came to visit; at any rate, she freely admitted at the end of her visit that the wisdom, wealth, and power of Solomon were even greater than she expected.

Basically, God made Solomon a genius in all fields in the known world; his inventions, insights, and peaceful and powerful reign caused him to be held in awe by other nations as he revolutionized the culture and commerce of the day. The fact that technologies suddenly developed with the Israeli and

Phoenician alliance around 1000 B.C. point to the life of a genius who "accelerated" their culture. The Bible clearly tells us the genius was Solomon.

ANCIENT TRADE ROUTES

If the ancients discovered America and the New World up to 2,500 years before Columbus, how would they have acquired the wisdom to do so? In Solomon's golden age of wisdom and expansion, a great deal of scientific knowledge was accumulated that was later lost, only to be rediscovered by the time of Columbus. Ecclesiastes, along with Proverbs and Isaiah, confirms the fact that the ancient peoples understood that worldwide trade winds moved in a circular pattern. The entire water cycle was also already known at that time—that the water of rivers flowing to oceans would evaporate, condense into water droplets, and furnish rain to replenish the inland rivers. There are remains of ancient civilizations that had visited vast parts of the world, including artifacts across the Americas from other nations besides the Native Americans.

> *The wind goes to the south and circles about to the north; it circles and circles about continually, and on its circuit the wind returns again* (Ecclesiastes 1:6 AMP).

> *When He prepared the heavens, I [Wisdom] was there; when He drew a circle upon the face of the deep and stretched out the firmament over it* (Proverbs 8:27 AMP).

This Scripture speaks of the earth's surface as being curved. Also, another Scripture points to this fact of a spherical earth in

Isaiah 40:22, *"It is He who sits above the circle of the earth, and its inhabitance are like grasshoppers."*

It is amazing that even the Polynesians, thousands of years ago, were able to accurately navigate across the Pacific Islands from Fiji to Hawaii—tiny dots amidst a million square miles of empty blue, which was considered ridiculous to the western mind. Even experienced western navigators with maps, sextant, and compass could never guarantee a landing, and they always said they sailed "toward" instead of "to" a place in hopes of reaching it. How could primitive Polynesians, without navigational equipment, accurately navigate to these islands with double-hulled canoes on long ocean voyages way before Columbus?

That they did so was proven by the voyages of the *Hokule'a*. Using only the stars, ocean currents (circular patterns), sea birds, and other natural signs, the *Hokule'a* has regularly made landfall in journeys from Hawaii to Tahiti and back. The voyaging canoe, *Hokule'a*, was named after the star that guides it on its journey back to Hawaii. In the Polynesian star map, Hawaii sits directly in line with the star Hokule'a. The knowledge of this star with the ability for such accurate voyages was preserved by the ancient navigators.[20]

Many of the world's inventions, especially in the area of transportation, can be traced to the wheel and to circular patterns. Once man rediscovered that the earth was not flat but circular, man advanced again.

The earth and the planets are circular and also rotate around the sun and on their own axes in a circular motion. Water moves in circular patterns. The Book of Ezekiel talks about the wheels of the living creatures moving as a wheel within a wheel, causing it to be able to move up and down, almost describing the helicopter or a hovercraft, and possibly an ancient blueprint for modern aircraft travel today.

> When the living creatures went, the wheels went beside them; and when the living creatures were lifted up from the earth, the wheels were lifted up. Wherever the spirit wanted to go, they went, because there the spirit went; and the wheels were lifted together with them, for the spirit of the living creatures was in the wheels (Ezekiel 1:19-20).

The wheels of a propeller along with the engines of an aircraft, both of which move in circular patterns, help cause the momentum for air travel. Even in the supernatural, circles create enough momentum to cause the invisible world to affect the visible world. In the Bible, the children of Israel circled the walls of Jericho and blew on the trumpets as they shouted when the walls came tumbling down. The Bible also says that the angels stand and worship around the throne or encircle the throne (see Rev. 5:11; 7:11). Photos taken in revival meetings almost always show the light around angelic beings as circular.

The Bible says that God wants His will done on earth as it is in Heaven. Humans and the earth were created in the likeness of Heaven and God. That means things in Heaven move in circular patterns as well. I believe as we praise and worship God and sense movement in the spirit realm, angelic hosts are moving around us in circular patterns, creating a type of whirlwind just as they do when worshiping *around* the throne.

Even Elijah was taken up in a whirlwind, which was another mode of transportation, taking him from this physical world to the supernatural world of Heaven (see 2 Kings 2:11). He would also often be transported on the earth from one location to another, causing his followers to walk a three days' journey before they could find his new location. In my book *Mysteries of the Glory Unveiled*, I explain how at times my wife and I have been transported from one location to another in our car while worshiping. Could it be the times that I and others have been physically transported from one physical location to another that it occurred while we were worshiping, causing a whirlwind effect in the Spirit that actually transported our physical bodies by spiritual circular trade winds over the earth?

The ancient world was far more advanced and interconnected than modern man has wanted to admit. During Solomon's time, the ancients knew far more than modern man did during the Dark Ages, when superstition, ignorance, and anti-Semitism reigned to such a point that many Christians, from the time of Constantine on, refused to read the Old Testament, referring to it as the book of the Jews.

By not having access to this wisdom, the modern world lost even the fact about the circular trade winds, which is talked about in the Bible. As modern man turned against the ancient people of Israel, the Jews, a loss of the ancient wisdom resulted. They even lost the knowledge of the New World, which, as some attest, ancient civilizations had already explored and visited.

THE GLORY OF THE ANCIENTS

The Bible mentions that *"all the earth sought the presence of Solomon...each man brought his present...at a set rate year by year"* (1 Kings 10:24-25). As leader of the triple alliance of Israel,

Egypt, and Phoenicia, Solomon was the head of the world's most powerful empire, which means that he not only had a hold on most of the maritime trading routes, but he also controlled the main critical overland trading routes.

Every king and nation had reason to get along with Solomon, who was the wisest, richest, and most powerful of his time—the nations around the earth sought the presence and favor of King Solomon with gifts. This is not to say that many of the kings did not genuinely like Solomon, like King Hiram of Phoenicia or the Queen of Sheba. The fact that the Bible states that royal gifts came in from the kings of the nations "year by year" implies an annual schedule that was predictable.

This most likely happened during the national feasts of great rejoicing that occurred during the Feast of Tabernacles. This feast had seven days of feasting climaxing in an eighth day (see Lev. 23:34-43); Solomon dismissed the happy crowds on the eighth day (1 Kings 8:66). The Feast of Tabernacles is also known as the Feast of the Nations. This was surely the Feast of Tabernacles referred to in First Kings 8:2: *"All the men of Israel assembled themselves unto King Solomon at the feast in the month of Ethanim, which is the seventh month."* The seventh month was the fall feast that lasted seven days, known as the Feast of Tabernacles.

> *And at that time Solomon held a feast, and all Israel with him, a great congregation, from the entering in of Hamath unto the river of Egypt, before the Lord our God, seven days and seven days, even fourteen days* (1 Kings 8:65 KJV).

49

"Even fourteen days" implies that Solomon started with the seven days but then doubled the feast, this time from seven days to fourteen days, as this was no ordinary Feast of Tabernacles, but one in which the glory of the Lord filled the Temple. First Kings 8:10 says, *"And it came to pass, when the priests came out of the holy place, that the cloud filled the house of the Lord."*

It seems very possible that Solomon invited the nations to Jerusalem during this feast year by year. People always brought their best gifts to the feasts of Israel, so this all seems very applicable and another foreshadowing of how things will be upon Messiah's return.

To this day in Israel, the spiritual leaders will pray for the nations of the world during this feast only at the Western Wall, as part of the prayers during this feast. Imagine if, that particular year when the glory filled the temple, kings of all nations were present to witness the event and then went back to tell the nations about the God of Israel and His glory.

Imagine many kings coming down the streets with their entourage of caravans loaded with precious gifts to the God of Israel via King Solomon. If the Israelites in alliance with the Phoenicians did visit the New World, then possibly some of Solomon's royal visitors could easily have come from the New World in the Americas. Remember the evidence that the tripartite alliance of Israel, Phoenicia, and Egypt produced trade routes that included the Pacific, Atlantic, and Indian Oceans, as well as the fact that the Bible says that kings from all the earth came to Jerusalem during this time.

Much of Solomon's reign is a foreshadowing of the reign of Jesus the Messiah when the King of kings reinstates the Feast of Tabernacles in Jerusalem at His return. Upon His return all nations, including Egypt, will be required to come up to Jerusalem to worship the Messiah during the Feast of Tabernacles. Zechariah 14:16-18 says:

> *And it shall come to pass that everyone who is left of all the nations which came against Jerusalem shall go up from year to year to worship the King, the Lord of hosts, and to keep the Feast of Tabernacles. And it shall be that whichever of the families of the earth do not come up to Jerusalem to worship the King, the Lord of hosts, on them there will be no rain. If the family of Egypt will not come up and enter in, they shall have no rain...*

The Messiah will rule, creating a time of worldwide peace, much like what occurred during Solomon's reign. Just as Solomon's reign was preceded by violent wars, so will the Messiah Jesus's reign be preceded by the most violent wars. Also, just as the world's wealth flowed to Jerusalem under King Solomon, the world's wealth will flow once again to Jerusalem each year, to King Jesus in Jerusalem (see 1 Kings 10:25; Isaiah 60:5-7).

When Solomon celebrated the dedication of the Temple, his most prized accomplishment, the ark of the covenant was placed within. There must have been many kings from the entire earth present; that particular Feast of Tabernacles was unlike any other.

> *And it came to pass, when the priests came out of the holy place, that the cloud filled the house of the Lord, so that the priests could not continue*

ministering because of the cloud; for the glory of the
Lord filled the house of the Lord (1 Kings 8:10-11).

This cloud was so powerful no human, including the priests, could stand in the Temple. Imagine what the visitors from other nations thought as the sense of awe and the fear of the Lord was in their midst. The kings of the earth no doubt extended the fame of Solomon and Israel to the entire world. Perhaps the knowledge and fame of the God of Israel spread even to the New World, if the cultural similarities some Native American tribes appear to have with Israel are any evidence.

All this began simply by Solomon giving a sacrificial offering to God and God asking Solomon what he wanted from Him. Solomon honored God by asking for wisdom. Instead, God gave him wisdom, wealth, power, and even allowed him to experience the glory cloud of the Lord. Unfortunately, Solomon's foreign wives began to influence him; toward the end of his life, he included idol worship in his kingdom, and the "golden age" of Israel began its decline.

People marveled at the wisdom of Jesus and Moses and connected their wisdom to the workings of miracles and signs and wonders. The term "wise men" has been attributed even to magicians in Babylon or to anyone who had wisdom and understanding of how the invisible world worked to effect physical miracles or manifestations.

Ask God to make you one of His wise men or women and to restore the ancient wisdom He has released on the earth for us to pick up once again. A good starting place for acquiring this wisdom is to ask God with a humble heart for the fear of the Lord and respect for His ancient people.

Chapter 3

A REVIVAL OF WISDOM

This chapter is taken from my book *Mysteries of the Glory Unveiled* **because of the relevant content within this context.**

And men of all nations, from all the kings of the earth who had heard of his wisdom, came to hear the wisdom of Solomon (1 KINGS 4:34).

With this new wave of signs and wonders, the Lord is releasing a new wave of wisdom, revelation, and knowledge. These are keys that allow us to venture into the untapped realms of glory in this new move of God, and as the miracles increase, so will the anointing of supernatural wisdom. This phenomenon will eventually become so powerful that people will come from all over the world just to hear the wisdom of God expressed, as they did in Solomon's day.

Through His prophet Habakkuk, God said, *"For the earth will be filled with the knowledge of the glory of the Lord, as the waters cover the sea"* (Hab. 2:14). This verse is often misquoted. We say that the earth will be filled with the glory of the Lord, rather than with the *knowledge* of the glory of the Lord. It is one thing to sense the glory in a meeting, and it is quite another thing to have the knowledge of that glory. When we have the knowledge, we not only sense the glory but we also have the keys to releasing miracles and manifestations from that glory.

Some may have wondered why at times they have sensed the glory, and yet they have never seen a physical manifestation of that glory. Having the knowledge of the glory makes the difference.

The glory could be likened to a cloud hovering over a city. The people see the cloud, but they lack the knowledge or wisdom necessary to make it rain. Clouds come and go sometimes without yielding rain. Now God is revealing to us the keys to releasing spiritual rain from the clouds of glory.

The apostle Paul knew the mysteries of revelation more than most men of his time, and this allowed him to tap into realms other men only dreamed of. It was this gift that enabled Paul to write more than half of the New Testament. He also walked in unusual miracles; he saw the third Heaven opened, and he received multitudes of other victories. Fortunately, Paul passed along some of these keys to us in his writings.

In Paul's prayer for the Ephesian believers, for instance, some of these keys are identified for us: *"making mention of you in my prayers: that the God of our Lord Jesus Christ, the Father of glory, may give to you the spirit of wisdom and revelation in the knowledge of Him"* (Eph. 1:16-17). "Wisdom," "revelation," and "knowledge" are keys that open the door to greater things in God. When we use these keys, we can expect to receive what lies behind the door: *"the eyes of your understanding being enlightened; that you may know what is the hope of His calling"* (Eph. 1:18).

Once you grasp a revelation of your calling in Him, then you can fully enter through its doorway with knowledge and wisdom. This is essential to walk into the frame that God has already prepared for your life.

SUPERNATURAL WISDOM UNLOCKS HEAVEN'S SUPPLIES

...what are the riches of the glory of His inheritance in the saints (Ephesians 1:18).

We know that in Heaven there is no lack. We also know, from these and other Scriptures, that we have an inheritance in Heaven. For instance, we will have perfect bodies when we get to Heaven, where there is no sickness. Because the Lord told us to pray, *"Your will be done on earth as it is in Heaven,"* we know that God can bring heavenly things to us here on earth (see Matt. 6:10).

When the same glory that is in Heaven comes down to earth, supernatural provision comes, and you can tap into your inheritance. Once you truly have a revelation that there is more than enough reserved for you in Heaven, you will no longer walk in lack—as long as you stay in the glory. This is why Jesus said,

> Do not lay up for yourselves treasures on earth, where moth and rust destroy and where thieves break in and steal; but lay up for yourselves treasures in heaven, where neither moth nor rust

destroys and where thieves do not break in and steal. For where your treasure is, there your heart will be also (Matthew 6:19-21).

If you can bring the glory of Heaven to the earth, then the treasures of Heaven will be manifested upon the earth. Just as healing, creative miracles, signs and wonders have been falling from Heaven as a result of the glory, so other heavenly things can come to us.

This is one of the reasons people have been experiencing new types of financial miracles in many of our meetings, such as money mysteriously appearing in wallets and purses and bank accounts as written about in my book *Mysteries of the Glory Unveiled*. This often happens right after someone has sown into the glory. God is showing us that Heaven has no lack.

When we understand this revelation, laying up treasure on earth becomes a much more risky proposition. If we lay up treasure in Heaven, we can make withdrawals from it whenever we get into the glory. When we do, we will find that it has multiplied 30-, 60-, and 100-fold. This is the best banking system in the world, and we don't even need an ATM card to access it.

In one of our services, the people came to the front to give spontaneously, but a man from Kenya had nothing to give. He told the Lord this, and the Lord said to him, *"I give seed to the sower."* Then the Lord told him to look in his wallet. There he found money that had not been there before. He went forward to give the money, and then he came to the microphone and testified about this miracle.

In this case, it was not a large amount, but God is also performing financial miracles for His people that are quite large, involving thousands and even millions of dollars. For example, just recently while we had another Glory Conference in Sedona, a man came up and offered to pay for all the expenses of our conference. This man, we later discovered, had $400 million worth of property that was held up internationally because the government was holding back releasing title deeds so he could sell off the property. The very next day he received a call from his lawyers that somehow the governor released the title deeds without going through all the red tape. Now he was free to sell off the condos and be a greater blessing to the ministry, not to mention save him from bankruptcy, as most of his money was tied up in that one investment.

During our Denver Outpouring in 2008, which lasted all summer and beyond, a woman gave an offering while the miracles and the glory were flowing. The next day another woman asked her to add up all her debts, which amounted to $60,000. She wrote a check to the woman so she could pay it all off. These types of testimonies are so numerous, occurring each week, that it would take an entire book to catalogue them.

Paul wrote, *"For we are His workmanship, created in Christ Jesus for good works, which God prepared beforehand that we should walk in them"* (Ephesians 2:10). The key to walking in them, when you are in the glory, is through revelation and knowledge. If we don't know (through revelation) that something exists, then we cannot walk in it. If no one told us that we had inherited $1 million from a long-lost relative, then we would not know where to go to claim it or even that we could claim it.

It is the same in the Spirit. When we receive the revelation that we actually have a great inheritance laid up for us (added to what we have been sowing into Heaven), then we can begin to unlock what has been reserved for us—through the golden keys of revelation and wisdom in the glory.

> For wisdom is a defense as money is a defense...
> (Ecclesiastes 7:12).

> Happy is the man who finds wisdom, and the man who gains understanding; for her proceeds are better than the profits of silver, and her gain than fine gold. She is more precious than rubies, and all the things you may desire cannot compare with her (Proverbs 3:13-15).

Why is wisdom greater than "profits" and greater than "all the things you may desire," meaning anything you could possibly want? Because if you have wisdom, you will have profits and anything else you need.

Many people think that the Bible instructs us not to have riches, but this is not true. It admonishes us not to seek gold and silver, but rather wisdom, so that we can tap into all the available riches for God's Kingdom. This is why the apostle Paul prayed for wisdom for the Ephesians. It is the key that allows us to tap into all the other dimensions of our inheritance.

When you are in need, don't just ask God to meet that specific need. Ask for wisdom, and you will know what to do to unlock more blessings. When presented with a choice, Solomon asked for wisdom from God. He knew this secret—with wisdom comes material blessing: *"Length of days is in her [wisdom's] right hand, in her left hand riches and honor"* (Prov. 3:16).

When Solomon asked for wisdom instead of gold and silver, fame and power, God gave him everything he lacked. He became the richest and most powerful man of his time. He was also known as the wisest, and as we have seen, men and women came from many places just to witness his great wisdom. It was wisdom that unlocked the rest of what Solomon needed.

Before God made the offer to Solomon that resulted in his receiving extraordinary wisdom, Solomon did something that began the entire process:

> *Now the king went to Gibeon to sacrifice there, for that was the great high place: Solomon offered a thousand burnt offerings on that altar* (1 Kings 3:4).

This very expensive offering made by Solomon was the thing that started his rise to wisdom and success. He sowed directly into the glory, using what little wisdom he had to bless God. This unlocked all of Heaven's resources.

God's response to this gift was sure: *"At Gibeon the Lord appeared to Solomon in a dream by night; and God said, 'Ask! What shall I give you?'"* (1 Kings 3:5).

Solomon was careful with his reply. He was very young to be a king, and he desperately needed wisdom to rule Israel. He could have asked for anything, but he asked for wisdom, and that gave him access to everything else. He prayed,

> *"Therefore give to Your servant an understanding heart to judge Your people, that I may discern between good and evil. For who is able to judge this great people of Yours?" The speech pleased the*

Lord, that Solomon had asked this thing (1 Kings 3:9-10).

When your prayers please the Lord, great favor can be shown to you, as it was to Solomon. Even when one is persecuted for pleasing God, it is also a form of God's favor because when you are persecuted for righteousness' sake or for pleasing God, the Word says, *"Great is your reward."* Either way, pleasing God in our prayers has great benefit and great reward both in this life and the age to come.

One of the lessons we learn from Solomon is that he did not pray flippantly, but showed the same (if not more) respect in God's presence as we would have if meeting an earthly president or king. Because of this, God was ready to bless him:

> *Then God said to him: "Because you have asked this thing, and have not asked long life for yourself, nor have asked riches for yourself, nor have asked the life of your enemies, but have asked for yourself understanding to discern justice, behold, I have done according to your words; see, I have given you a wise and understanding heart.... And I have also given you what you have not asked: both riches and honor, so that there shall not be anyone like you among the kings all your days"* (1 Kings 3:11-13).

Asking God for an anointing of wisdom pleases Him and may result in a special revival of supernatural wisdom. This is clearly what happened with Solomon, and "men of all nations" heard of his wisdom and traveled to Jerusalem to witness it personally.

SUPERNATURAL WISDOM LOOSES MIRACLES

Paul prayed for wisdom for the Ephesians because he knew that this gift unlocks new realms of the glory. Paul prayed that they would know *"what is the exceeding greatness of His power toward us who believe, according to the working of His mighty power"* (Eph. 1:19).

Another realm that wisdom unlocks is the realm of miracles. What does this phrase, "according to the working of His mighty power," really mean to us? God is not only turning up the power and increasing the glory, but He is giving us the knowledge of His glory. He is teaching us the inner workings of His mighty power. He is giving us keys that will unleash the greatest miracles ever recorded. Even when Jesus performed miracles through wisdom, they said of Jesus, *"And what wisdom is this which is given to Him, that such mighty works are performed by His hands"* (Mark 6:2). Jesus was our model using the wisdom of God to unleash the power of God.

What does wisdom have to do with miracles? Everything! Wisdom and revelation knowledge are the keys to the miracle realm.

Once when I was praying for a boy with a paralyzed arm, the Lord told me to sing the prayer. As I sang, the glory began to come, and the boy was instantly healed.

When a fellow minister was asked to pray for a mentally challenged boy, he asked the Lord what to do. The Lord told him to make the boy run with him. He could not understand how running could heal the boy's mind, but he obeyed. The wisdom of God is greater than our human reasoning. As he ran with the boy, the boy's mind was healed.

Later, God explained the principle behind this act. Before a person acts, he or she must think. In this case, however, God made the boy act first, and then his mind caught up with his action. The key was simply listening to the wisdom or revelation of God and obeying it instantly—whether or not it made sense at the time.

Jesus moved in miracle power through wisdom:

> *And when the Sabbath had come, He began to teach in the synagogue. And many hearing Him were astonished, saying, "Where did this Man get these things? And what wisdom is this which is given to Him, that such mighty works are performed by His hands!"* (Mark 6:2)

And again,

> *Where did this Man get this wisdom and these mighty works?* (Matthew 13:54)

When Jesus performed miracles, people noticed that He possessed great wisdom. There has always been a direct connection between wisdom and miracles.

The apostle Paul also moved in great miracles:

> *Now God worked unusual miracles by the hands of Paul, so that even handkerchiefs or aprons were brought from his body to the sick, and the diseases left them and the evil spirits went out of them* (Acts 19:11-12).

Paul had seized upon the revelation that all he needed was a point of contact to release the power of God upon the sick and suffering. He knew that if he was limited to the laying on of hands, he could not reach everyone. He therefore used aprons or prayer cloths to release the power of God and reach out to people he could not personally visit for miracles, healings, and deliverances. Thanks to that revelation, we now know that people can be healed when we pray for them over the telephone, or even when they are watching a minister on television.

Many television ministers often tell the people watching their program to lay hands on their television sets to receive healing. Somewhere along the line, we received the revelation that all people needed was a point of contact to release their faith. We do not always have to personally lay hands on them or call them out during one of our crusades or meetings in order for them to be healed.

During a six-month revival in Paris, we used prayer cloths to reach people who couldn't come to the meetings. Many were healed of cancer, leukemia, and other sicknesses, and some of them were on the other side of the world.

Some even put these cloths under the pillows of mentally tormented people, and they were freed. Women put them under the pillows of their unsaved husbands, and the conviction of the Holy Spirit worked on them all through the night. One simple revelation can revolutionize an entire move of God.

Stephen, the martyr, moved in great miracles, and he also had an unusual gift of wisdom:

> And Stephen, full of faith and power, did great wonders and signs among the people.... And they were not able to resist the wisdom and the Spirit by which he spoke (Acts 6:8,10).

God used Moses to perform some of the greatest miracles, signs, and wonders ever recorded, and he was also a man learned in all wisdom: *"And Moses was learned in all the wisdom of the Egyptians, and was mighty in words and deeds"* (Acts 7:22).

We know that true wisdom comes from God and that worldly wisdom is only a perverted reflection of the true thing. Here again, however, we see a connection between wisdom and the miracle-working power of God.

Daniel moved in remarkable wisdom, and he also displayed the power of God to the Babylonians:

> *And in all matters of wisdom and understanding about which the king examined them, he found them ten times better than all the magicians and astrologers who were in all his realm* (Daniel 1:20).

Again we find a direct connection between wisdom and moving in miracles and the supernatural. Daniel's wisdom surpassed that of the sorcerers of his day. Their wisdom failed the critical test: *"Then the king gave the command to call the magicians, the astrologers, the sorcerers, and the Chaldeans to tell the king his dreams..."* (Dan. 2:2).

It is interesting to note that even in Bible days, those who moved in the supernatural—whether they were on God's side or not—were often called "wise men," as these men in Babylon were (see Dan. 2:12-14). Why would magicians, astrologers, sorcerers, and the like be called "wise men"? It was because the people of that day recognized a direct connection between wisdom and miraculous powers.

Satan's wisdom is always limited, and these so-called "wise men" could not interpret the king's dream. This angered the king, and he ordered them to be executed. Their lives were spared only because Daniel had the wisdom to interpret the dream:

> *Therefore Daniel went to Arioch, whom the king had appointed to destroy the wise men of Babylon. He went and said thus to him: "Do not destroy the wise men of Babylon; take me before the king, and I will tell the king the interpretation"* (Daniel 2:24).

> *Then the secret was revealed to Daniel in a night vision. So Daniel blessed the God of heaven. Daniel answered and said: "Blessed be the name of God forever and ever, for wisdom and might are His.... He gives wisdom to the wise and knowledge to those who have understanding. He reveals deep and secret things..."* (Daniel 2:19-22).

When the Lord spoke the worlds into being, wisdom was there with Him, the tool He used to bring about the first creative miracles ever recorded:

> *The Lord by wisdom founded the earth; by understanding He established the heavens; by His knowledge the depths were broken up, and clouds drop down the dew* (Proverbs 3:19-20).

The same tool of wisdom, used by God when creating the heavens and the earth, is available to us today.

Wisdom, understanding, and knowledge were actually created before the earth was created. Wisdom was (and still is) the tool God uses to perform creative miracles:

The Lord possessed me at the beginning of His way, before His works of old. I have been established from everlasting, from the beginning, before there was ever an earth.... While as yet He had not made the earth or the fields, or the primal dust of the world. When He prepared the heavens, I was there (Proverbs 8:22-23,26-27).

In the beginning, God created the heavens and the earth, but before the beginning, He created wisdom. Wisdom was His servant working behind the scenes: *"Then I was beside Him as a master craftsman; and I was daily His delight"* (Prov. 8:30), and Jeremiah says, *"He has made the earth by His power, He has established the world by His wisdom"* (Jer. 10:12).

Ask God for the spirit of wisdom so you can tap into the power of creative miracles. Then thank Him for this priceless gift with a prayer of thankfulness, as did Daniel:

I thank You and praise You, O God of my fathers; You have given me wisdom and might, and have now made known to me what we asked of You... (Daniel 2:23).

SUPERNATURAL WISDOM RAISES THE DEAD

The Father of glory, may give to you the spirit of wisdom and revelation in the knowledge of Him... which He worked in Christ when He raised Him from the dead (Ephesians 1:17,20).

In the summer of 1999, when I was preaching the final night of a series of meetings in Montreal, Canada, in the church pastored by Pierre Cyr, something exciting happened. A spirit of revelation and wisdom came upon me in the middle of the sermon. Although I did not have time to search out doctrinally what God was showing me, He told me to share it.

I was preaching about Ezekiel in the valley of dry bones. God had told him to raise the bones up by the spoken word. When you say what God is saying, something happens. Ezekiel was commanded to do this, and he was promised that his words would bring life. He was told to say: *"Thus says the Lord God to these bones: 'Surely I will cause breath to enter into you, and you shall live'"* (Ezek. 37:5). The moment Ezekiel said what God said, something happened: *"So I prophesied as I was commanded; and as I prophesied, there was a noise, and suddenly a rattling; and the bones came together, bone to bone"* (Ezek. 37:7).

As I was speaking in Montreal, I suddenly saw something very clearly. It seemed so simple that I wondered why I had never seen it before. The next verse says: *"Indeed, as I looked, the sinews and the flesh came upon them, and the skin covered them over; but there was no breath in them"* (Ezek. 37:8).

I suddenly realized how the dead were raised. I was reading from the French Bible, and it used the word *spirit* instead of the word *breath*. The same Hebrew word was being translated two slightly different ways.

The bones of these dead people were now covered with flesh, but they were still dead. The reason this was true is explained in this verse: *"There was no spirit in them."* When a person dies, his or her human spirit (that God has given to each person) departs into Heaven or hell. The only way a dead body can rise again is if the spirit of that person comes back into his or her body. With that in mind, look at the next two verses:

Also He said to me, "Prophesy to the breath [spirit], prophesy, son of man, and say to the breath [spirit], 'Thus says the Lord God: "Come from the four winds, O breath [spirit], and breathe on these slain, that they may live."'" So I prophesied as He commanded me, and breath [spirit] came into them, and they lived, and stood upon their feet, an exceedingly great army (Ezekiel 37:9-10).

Having the knowledge of how spiritual things work helps greatly when it comes time to obey God in such a case. The human spirit of a person will revive the dead body. The spirit of a person is the real person (that lives eternally), not the flesh.

It was after sharing this revelation that I prophesied over Luigi, a fellow evangelist, that he would raise the dead. Armed with this revelation, he did it just a week later. When he saw his opportunity, he shouted out to the corpse, "Spirit of life, come into her!" At that moment, the woman opened her eyes and returned to life.

The first account of resurrection power in the Bible was found in the Garden shortly after God created the earth: *"And the Lord God formed man of the dust of the ground, and breathed into his nostrils the breath [spirit] of life; and man became a living being"* (Gen. 2:7).

Even though man had been formed, he needed one more ingredient—a spirit. Life is in the spirit. God breathed a portion of Himself into man, and man lived.

Elisha walked in this same wisdom and revelation glory, and he also raised the dead:

When Elisha came into the house, there was the child, lying dead on his bed. He went in therefore, shut the door behind the two of them, and prayed to the Lord. And he went up and lay on the child, and put his mouth on his mouth, his eyes on his eyes, and his hands on his hands; and he stretched himself out on the child, and the flesh of the child became warm (2 Kings 4:32-34).

I believe that when Elisha put his mouth on the mouth of the child, he literally breathed into the boy. We see in the previous verse that he had sent his servant, Gehazi, and told him to put his staff on the face of the child, but this did not produce the desired effect. When the prophet himself came and stretched himself out upon the child, the breath, or spirit, of the boy came back into him. This was symbolic of the way in which God created us in His image.

Elisha stayed in the glory until the work was complete:

He returned and walked back and forth in the house, and again went up and stretched himself out on him; then the child sneezed seven times, and the child opened his eyes (2 Kings 4:35).

Here is a principle for us to consider. In emergency situations, when someone is unconscious, his spirit begins to leave him. When this happens, mouth-to-mouth resuscitation is frequently used to revive the person. The word *resuscitation* is related in meaning to the word *resurrection*. Mouth-to-mouth resuscitation works to revive some who have already died or who are in the process of dying. God seems to honor this prophetic act, even when performed by unbelievers.

This is not to say that all dead people will be raised if we breathe into them. It is simply a prophetic sign that gives us an understanding about how things work in the Spirit. That said, though, I am convinced that in the days ahead the raising of the dead to life again will be one of the most common manifestations marking the last-day move of God. The Lord has shown me that whole groups of people will even be raised from the dead as a simple servant of the Lord commands breath or their spirit to return to them.

These dead perhaps will have died through war, disease, terrorist attacks, or natural disasters, but that's not the important thing. What is important is that God is empowering His people with wisdom to raise the dead. Very soon now the raising of the dead will even be caught on television as a sign to the world of the power of our God. We are entering the last days, the Elijah/Jesus dispensation.

When the glory comes, ask God to manifest His glory in the raising of the dead. Listen for revelation and wisdom that He may whisper into your ear. The raising of the dead is the glory of God manifested, as it was with the raising of Jesus's friend Lazarus:

> *When Jesus heard that, He said, "This sickness is not unto death, but for the glory of God, that the Son of God may be glorified through it." ...Jesus said to her, "Did I not say to you that if you would believe you would see the glory of God?"* (John 11:4,40)

Part of seeing the glory of God, therefore, is seeing the dead among us raised to life. Jesus gave us an example when He raised Lazarus from the dead, but we can still see these same miracles today.

SUPERNATURAL WISDOM RELEASES AUTHORITY

...and seated Him at His right hand in the heavenly places, far above all principality and power and might and dominion, and every name that is named, not only in this age but also in that which is to come. And He put all things under His feet, and gave Him to be head over all things to the church (Ephesians 1:20-22).

Authority comes from a supernatural revelation. God is giving us revelation concerning our speaking to those in authority in the world in any and every sphere of influence. Just as the apostles and prophets of old stood before world rulers, so God is putting upon us both the burden and the revelation to speak to the rulers of this world as a testimony before the end. As the glory increases, the favor of God will come on many for these crucially important tasks.

As we have seen, Isaiah foretold,

Arise, shine; for your light has come! And the glory of the Lord is risen upon you.... The Gentiles shall come to your light, and kings to the brightness of your rising (Isaiah 60:1,3).

Jesus walked in this authority. When He was just beginning His ministry, and the men of Nazareth wanted to throw Him off a cliff, He escaped into the crowd (see Luke 4:28-30). They could not take Him before His time. He knew that the authority He had from His Father was greater than any authority of man.

Later, the disciples would escape when they were imprisoned and continue to do the will of the Lord until their time had come. I believe that we should exercise our God-given authority more often, and when we have a revelation of who we are in Christ, we can.

DECLARING THE KINGDOM

An airline employee gave me a ticket to fly to a conference in Dallas (where I was also to have a television interview on Daystar Television). When I checked in at the ticket counter, the agent entered the information into the computer and then told me that the ticket I had was not valid. The employee who gave it to me had apparently changed departments, she said. I asked her to check again because I had just talked to my friend, and he had told me it was good. She insisted that it was not.

I went to the back of the line to ponder what I should do next. The flight would be leaving soon. "What should I do, Lord?" I prayed.

The Lord told me to take the flight, so I went back to the counter and asked the woman to please check again. She became a little irritated, told me that I shouldn't even have that ticket in my possession, and asked me to return it to her.

I went back to where I had left my bags to get the ticket, and as I did, I again asked the Lord what I should do. He said to me, "I told you to take the plane, not to ask a second opinion. This is My airport, and you are My ambassador. Go on up, and take the flight."

With my ticket in hand, I quickly made my way to the departure gate. At the gate, the same thing happened. The agent typed my information into the computer, and then she said, "I see that you already started to check in downstairs. Your ticket is invalid. What are you doing here?"

I answered that I really needed to take this flight and that there must have been a mistake. She proceeded to call the lady downstairs, and I began to pray for the favor of God and to declare, "The Kingdom of Heaven is at hand." I was thinking of Jesus's command to the disciples: *"And as you go, preach, saying, 'The kingdom of heaven is at hand.' Heal the sick, cleanse the lepers, raise the dead, cast out demons. Freely you have received, freely give"* (Matt. 10:7-8).

In these verses, we can see an obvious connection between the declaration of the Kingdom of Heaven and seeing the power of God displayed in mighty miracles. I was believing God to overrule the airline's decision and to get me on that flight.

Suddenly the agent changed her mind and hung up. "Oh," she said, "it's probably one of those lazy workers sending us more work up here." Then she gave me my boarding passes, coming and going. I had a great time in the conference in Dallas and in the television interview with Marcus and Joni Lamb.

Immediately after the interview, I went to see my father before flying back to Phoenix. A recently certified doctor of alphabiotics, he was in a health food store adjusting people's necks and backs, something he does as a side career. The Lord told me to pray for the people he was working on. I asked him if it would be all right, and he agreed. I told the people, "Jesus is going to heal you."

"Is this a new technique?" they asked. I told them it was.

As I prayed, legs grew, and backs and necks popped into place. The shoppers in the store were in awe of what God was doing, and many stepped out of the line to buy their health food products and got in line for an adjustment. The glory of God suddenly electrified the store.

The owners also came to see what was happening. At first, I thought they would stop me, but they seemed to be frozen with surprise, their mouths open. The Lord whispered to me, "The Kingdom of Heaven is at hand." I felt total freedom, as if I were in one of my own meetings.

After the people received free adjustments from Jesus, I began to minister to them spiritually. A German stewardess involved in the New Age movement received the Lord as her Savior. I approached the cashier and began to prophesy to her, revealing things in her past that God wanted to mend. She wept loudly.

The glory filled the place, and it was an awesome experience. It was not so much the fact that there were a few miraculous healings, but rather that the Kingdom, or government, of God had taken over the place—because of the glory of the Lord. It happened because I received a revelation from God of my authority in Him.

SEATED WITH CHRIST

The Bible shows us that we are seated with Christ in heavenly places (see Eph. 2:6). Since there is no distance in the glory, we are as near to Heaven as we are to anything here on earth. When we are in the glory and we speak to people, we are speaking from the position where Christ has seated us in heavenly places. Therefore, people will recognize our authority. If we speak only from our position here on the earth (without the glory), then our words cannot carry the same weight. The glory represents the weight of God's authority, and kings and others in authority recognize authority when they see it.

This same glory took the simple fisherman Peter and made him into an ambassador for the King of kings. From then on, people of great worldly authority recognized Peter's heavenly authority.

When Peter denied Jesus, he no longer walked in that same authority, and he feared even a simple woman who questioned him. On the Day of Pentecost, however, after the Holy Spirit had fully come, Peter preached to the very people he had feared only days before. The difference was that he had been touched by a new dimension of glory and had recovered his heavenly authority.

In the realm of authority, everything is done by revelation and wisdom. Once you get a revelation of your seat in the heavenly places and you walk in that glory, it is no longer you speaking, but Christ in you. All authority stems from revelation in the glory, and we are experiencing a revival of that holy wisdom.

Paul, who wrote the letter to the Ephesians, knew this authority well. He spoke to religious and governmental leaders with great authority. When he was a prisoner on a ship, and the Lord showed him that the ship was about to be wrecked, he still had his authority. He told the captain of the ship what God's instructions were to save the people on board. When Paul made it safely to an island, everyone on the island was healed, including the governor of the island. The gospel was preached on that island through this prisoner.

Paul spent time in chains, but this did not diminish his authority. He called himself an ambassador in chains and still continued to lead the churches in his apostolic authority. He did not even fear Nero, the leader of the Roman Empire, who could have had him killed on any whim. Paul said, *"For to me, to live is Christ, and to die is gain. But if I live on in the flesh, this will mean fruit from my labor; yet what I shall choose I cannot tell"* (Phil. 1:21-22).

Paul had the authority to choose; therefore, he did not fear the authority of Nero. He knew that release, death, or imprisonment was a decision between him and God. Basically, Paul was saying, "God and I are working on this decision of whether I should stay or go. Once we have made up our minds, Nero, we will let you know what you are allowed to do with me." Until then, the apostle continued his writing ministry from prison. That is the power of the authority that comes with supernatural wisdom.

When Paul and Silas were in prison, they began to worship the Lord. As they did, the glory came in and shook the place (see Acts 16:25-26). The Kingdom of the Lord took priority over the authority of the Roman Empire, the guard and his family received the Lord, and Paul and Silas went on their way preaching to others.

Jesus walked in this same authority when He was threatened and mocked. He knew that the only authority his accusers had was the authority His Father had given them. He went on to tell His disciples to declare that the Kingdom of Heaven was at hand everywhere they went. What they were declaring was that the rules of the world's system now had to bow to a higher rule. The new king was Jesus, and His rules were above all other rules—including those of the Roman Empire.

When Moses went to the Pharaoh and said to him, "Let my people go!" he was also declaring that the Kingdom of his God was greater than the kingdom of Egypt.

When Daniel was told that a new rule in Babylon forbade anyone from praying to another God, and that anyone caught disobeying the rule would be executed, he continued praying three times a day as if that rule did not apply to him. Because he prayed with his windows open toward Jerusalem, the other governors and satraps could hear him (see Dan. 6:10). (Whether or not he did it purposely so that he could be heard is open to debate, but his windows were clearly open and he could be heard as he prayed toward Jerusalem, not bowing down to the new law.)

When Daniel was taken to the lions' den, he still had his authority intact. He showed that he would never bow down to other gods, and that he believed his God would deliver him. This moved even the king. This authority was a result of Daniel having received wisdom from Heaven.

In the lions' den, the glory of the Lord was with Daniel, and the rules of Heaven applied. In the glory, in Heaven, and in the Garden before the fall, animals did not kill humans. The act of animals turning on the crowning glory of God's creation was a result of the fall. Since the glory of Heaven filled the lions' den, the lions acted accordingly. They no longer remembered that they enjoyed eating human flesh, because it was not normal in the glory and in the Kingdom of Heaven.

Jesus taught us to pray, *"Your kingdom come. Your will be done on earth as it is in heaven"* (Matt. 6:10). When Heaven's glory comes to earth, you can declare that the Kingdom of

Heaven is at hand. And when you do, even the forces of nature must bow.

When David confronted Goliath, he was still very young. But he already had a revelation of his position seated in heavenly places. He had spent hours worshiping the Lord as the glory came down while he tended his father's sheep. When he heard the intimidating report concerning Goliath, it did not faze him. He went to Goliath with his heavenly authority and declared the victory that he had already seen in the glory. He did not look at his own size, age, or experience apart from the Lord (see 1 Sam. 17:33-37). He knew that he had a covenant and a promise from God and that the giant did not.

God backed David up. Because Saul, a much larger man, did not have a revelation of his position in the glory, he was often insecure and frightened. David was never afraid.

EXERCISING KINGDOM AUTHORITY

Some years ago, we were trying to extend my wife's stay in France as we were ministering there often in those days, and the official serving us was giving us a hard time. She insisted that my wife's birth certificate had to be officially translated into French before they could issue her any new papers.

Since we needed the papers that day, we didn't have time to have that translation work completed. The woman left us for a few minutes, and I began to pray. I commanded that the authority of the French government bow its knee to the Kingdom of Heaven and treat us as ambassadors. In a little while, the woman returned and asked me if I wanted two copies or three of the needed document. It seemed as if she had completely forgotten the problem, and she gave us exactly what we needed.

The Kingdom of Heaven, the glory, is at hand, and God's promise will be quickly fulfilled: *"The earth will be filled with the knowledge of the glory of the Lord, as the waters cover the sea"* (Hab. 2:14). This is not to be confused with the popular teaching held by some that we will set up ourselves a kingdom and stay put right here, nor is it an excuse to disobey the laws of the land on a whim. This revelation takes us far beyond those carnal concepts and empowers us for greatness to glorify God in this present world.

SUPERNATURAL WISDOM BRINGS FAVOR BEFORE GREAT MEN

Wisdom and favor go together when it comes to speaking with world leaders, and both come from having revelation of the glory. Joseph walked in such wisdom and favor that it brought him eventually into the presence of the king:

> *And the patriarchs, becoming envious, sold Joseph into Egypt. But God was with him and delivered him out of all his troubles, and gave him favor and wisdom in the presence of Pharaoh, king of Egypt; and he made him governor over Egypt and all his house* (Acts 7:9-10).

When the Kingdom of Heaven is understood and declared or preached, the atmosphere changes. The revelation that the Kingdom of Heaven is here brings in that greater glory. When you declare what God is declaring, it begins to manifest wherever you are. Any place can be invaded with the glory of the Kingdom of Heaven, and every authority must bow to that Kingdom.

Philip went into a region where Simon the sorcerer was influential. People respected the man. When Philip came into town, however, the tables were turned:

> *And they heeded him [Simon] because he had aston-ished them with his sorceries for a long time. But when they believed Philip as he preached the things concerning the kingdom of God and the name of Jesus Christ, both men and women were baptized. Then Simon himself also believed; and when he was baptized he continued with Philip, and he was amazed, seeing the miracles and signs which were done (Acts 8:11-13).*

As God is bringing new signs and wonders upon the church, He is also giving us the favor and revelation to speak to any and all who are in authority so we can reach many more people for God's glory.

Alberto Motessi, an Argentine evangelist, preaches in crusades all over South America. There he fills stadiums with hundreds of thousands of people. He has often been called the "Evangelist to the Presidents," for he has spoken with and led more presidents to the Lord than any other minister in South America. This is due to two elements: the simple favor and wisdom of God upon his life, and the great compassion he has for lost souls—whether they are presidents or homeless men and women on the street.

Ruth Ward Heflin walked in this same wisdom, glory, and favor to speak to leaders. She spoke to many U.S. leaders, including the President of the United States, and to officials at the Pentagon. Doors opened for her in many different countries as well to speak and prophesy to presidents and other high-ranking officials due to revelation of her authority in the heavenly places. She knew that when God told her to speak to the head of some government, the door would open—even though she might not have known anyone in that particular government.

The apostle Paul had the same revelation. Even in chains he spoke to Governor Felix, and convicted him of sin. Felix admitted that he had been deeply influenced by Paul (see Acts 24:22-27). Paul eventually appealed to Caesar and was determined to speak to the leaders of the great empire in Rome. He ended his days in Rome, having spoken to many leaders and having influenced the entire known world for Christ.

John the Baptist had the same authority when he spoke, as did many other mighty men and women of God, both in the Bible and in the annals of history.

The preaching of the Kingdom of Heaven is one of the greatest last-day revelations and one the church has yet to fully understand and apply. The wisdom and knowledge of God is being revealed to us so we can walk in the fullness of what has been reserved for us from the beginning. Jesus told us to use wisdom in the glory when speaking to rulers: *"Therefore be wise as serpents and harmless as doves"* (Matt. 10:16).

God is still extending His favor to the church. Whether your country is favorable to Christianity or indifferent, or if people are being thrown in prison and persecution has begun, the same glory applies. There have been seasons in which the church has prospered and grown in favor with God and man, and there have been times of great persecution. Supernatural wisdom to speak to kings is not limited to ideal situations. The rulers of the world are subject to the glory of God when it manifests on the earth through you—whatever the situation. God is looking for those He can use to speak to kings, for they wait to hear the word of the Lord.

Jesus promised us that this opportunity would arise: *"You will be brought before governors and kings for My sake, as a testimony to them and to the Gentiles"* (Matt. 10:18). What do you say when God gives you an audience with a president, a banker, a judge, a police officer, a general, an actor, a warlock? You will only speak and do what you hear and see your Father in Heaven saying and doing. Whatever comes from the throne will be backed by the authority and power of Heaven. Jesus said,

> *But when they deliver you up, do not worry about how or what you should speak. For it will be given to you in that hour what you should speak; for it is not you who speak, but the Spirit of your Father who speaks in you* (Matthew 10:19-20).

Adam and Eve had authority over every living thing—as long as the glory of God was in the Garden. They lost this authority in the fall. Now that God's glory is being restored, so is our authority and favor with others. I believe that God will give you personal revelation and favor to speak to those in authority whom He has put on your heart.

Some of you will speak to presidents and heads of nations and bring them a timely word from the Lord. Some will be used as Esther, to change the heart of the king in favor of the Lord's people. And some of you will be used to open entire countries to the gospel.

Many souls will be saved as a result of these efforts. Ask God for supernatural wisdom, and then do exactly as He tells you. His Word declares,

> *If any of you lacks wisdom, let him ask of God, who gives to all liberally and without reproach, and it will be given to him. But let him ask in faith, with no doubting, for he who doubts is like a wave of the sea driven and tossed by the wind* (James 1:5-6).

Make that promise yours today, and you will find your authority increasing proportionally.

Chapter 4

ANCIENT GEOGRAPHICAL PORTALS

There are ancient geographical locations still on the earth today where the gateway or portal to Heaven was once opened in ancient times and is still open to those who access those gateways. These open portals allow greater access into the supernatural, making it easier to access Heaven, revelation, and heavenly encounters as one is able to access a highway of the supernatural that ancient men of God paved for us through their encounters with God in those very places.

This is not to negate the fact that the Kingdom of God is around us and with us at all times, but there are also ladders and grids from Heaven to earth that have been set up and are still there. Sometimes an open Heaven exists to such a degree that the moment you step into the vicinity of that location and begin to connect you are already whisked up into that realm. On a local level, a church in full-blown revival would have easier access to Heaven than a dead church where one has to lay the groundwork all over again to open up the heavens over that particular place.

The ancient men of God knew where some of these locations already were, and others created new ones that today are still open; in these places, dreams, visions, clarity in hearing God, fresh revelation, angelic encounters, and the glory of God are already present.

I believe the place with the most open Heaven portals per capita on the face of the earth is located in the tiny land of Israel. It has more geographical supernatural highways connecting it to Heaven than any other nation in the world, and it is the most overlooked. Often, the greatest secrets are hidden for those who seek God and search it out. Of all the geographical portals in Israel, the largest one is in Jerusalem. Nations from around the world would come here to meet with God, and here the glory of God showed up thousands of years before Jesus died and rose again. Jerusalem is also the most overlooked place for encounters with God, largely due to current events and the Israeli-Palestinian conflict.

When the Romans destroyed Jerusalem in A.D. 70, the Roman soldiers recorded that a blue flame of the Lord began to rise out of the ruined Temple in Jerusalem, astonishing them all. It began to ascend for a few weeks on the Mount of Olives until it finally lifted. This tangible sign of the glory and power of God rested in Jerusalem so that even pagan Romans standing inside that geographical portal could see it. As the Romans destroyed the Temple, killing most of the Jews or taking them captive outside of Jerusalem, the blue flame of the Lord lifted until their return to Jerusalem years later.

Recently, while doing evangelistic miracle meetings in Jamaica, the blue flame of the Lord appeared. On the last night the power of God shook the place with many creative miracles and deliverances. One girl, whose mother was a witch, seemed to have embodied the actual principality of witchcraft over the city. When she was finally set free, the glory exploded even greater. Souls were saved all over the place.

As we entered the room of our hotel 30 minutes away, the lights and the power of the entire region began to flicker off and on for quite awhile. The Lord began to tell me that the last night's meeting knocked down the principality. I discovered that after we left at about 3:00 a.m., people on the streets looked up to the sky and saw a blue lightning-like flame strike the earth and even the transformers, but they did not get consumed. The spiritual and physical power grid of the city had been touched by the greater power of God. People began to hit the dirt and repent of their sins, including many who were in the occult. This led to a wave of more souls being saved for weeks after those meetings.

The portal from Heaven to earth had been opened up over that city, and the blue flame of the Lord also appeared as a sign. Also, I believe the Lord, through the meetings there, disrupted the demonic gateway or highway into the demonic. It all started when we declared, "The Kingdom and government of Heaven now takes over the demonic stronghold of this city."

THE CENTRALITY OF JERUSALEM

God chose to call Jerusalem His earthly footstool. He also speaks of Jerusalem constantly throughout the Bible as the place He chooses to let His presence and glory abide, as far as a physical location. It is where the Upper Room, as well as many other encounters, occurred. Also, it is the place where His Son Jesus died and rose from the dead. It is where dead bodies rose out of their graves when the earth shook as Jesus was dying. It is also the place that the Bible says the Messiah will return to set up His earthly Kingdom during the millennium (see Isa. 2:2-4). It is a place definitely set apart as a geographical location where one can meet with God apart from all the religiosity that may also exist there.

Once a portal has been opened over a place, a permanent door exists there that may be reopened more easily: a door does not need to be created again. One must first go back to the ancient pathways and then watch God reopen it.

Why do you think that almost every major religion has a presence of some kind in Jerusalem? The Mormons have a large headquarters there along with the Muslims, Catholics, and many other religions and groups. Because the enemy also tries to take over the portal, he likes to camp out there too. Whoever dominates the portal also gets a certain worldwide power and authority. More journalists are based in Jerusalem than any other city. More battles in history have been fought over this one small city than any other city in the world, even though it has no known natural commodity, waterway, or earthly value. But because of its spiritual importance, even the antichrist will eventually try to seat himself in Jerusalem in an unsuccessful bid to close the portal for good and be worshiped as God.

In fact, the most expensive and valued real estate in the world will still be Jerusalem when the Messiah returns and sets up His Kingdom with the New Jerusalem overlapping the earthly Jerusalem. Nations from around the world will come.

Many people forget about present-day Jerusalem because they think the New Jerusalem will replace it. Rather, the two Jerusalems are connected in the same way that Jacob's ladder represents the connection that exists between Heaven and earth.

I have had many open Heaven and third Heaven encounters and visitations in Israel and in Jerusalem. Many of my friends in ministry and in the Lord have also experienced these encounters. The first time we had gone into the Upper Room ourselves, we had a very powerful encounter that changed our lives and ministry. It altered the entire course of my life from that day onward as I started to connect my life with Heaven from that gateway in Jerusalem in the Upper Room.

I really needed that open portal to give me a head start in the things of the supernatural. From that day in 1994 until now, we have been flung into the ministry of revival, as revivals broke out in our ministry afterward with ever-increasing miracles, healings, signs, and salvations. The meetings sometimes last from four weeks to six months in the same place. Entering that ancient portal changed my life.[21]

Of course you have to seek it, desire it, and ask in faith. Someone can just as easily stand there and have nothing happen if they are not looking for anything. In a similar way, when a major revival breaks out in a place, it is possible for one person to stand next to another person who is being miraculously touched and remain totally disconnected. I believe you need to purpose in your heart that you are going to connect with God when in those places.

BETHEL: THE GATE OF HEAVEN

Bethel is another place where we, and the teams we have brought with us, have had many encounters with the glory of God. Jacob describes Bethel in Genesis 28:17 as the house of God, and the gate of heaven. Again, we see the idea of a permanent spiritual gateway—a permanent open Heaven over a geographical location.

When our team went just a few years ago, the following occurred. We went to the spot where we believe Jacob actually had his encounter. We were supernaturally led there by the Lord when we were lost in Bethel one day; at that time, our driver said to us, "Just go pray over there." That place is also believed to be the correct location of Jacob's encounter by the local settlers.

We had a group from Dubai with us, which was amazing in itself. One of the men of God from Dubai had a direct encounter with Jesus at Bethel and was told great and mighty things that are already starting to occur in his life and ministry. After he had the entire encounter, he was so overwhelmed he began to wonder if it was just all in his mind. He wanted it to be real but feared it was his imagination.

During that time his pastor, who is also from Dubai, entered the same vision. In his encounter, he was able to watch his friend in the Spirit visit with Jesus; he then saw him doubting the visitation and asking God if it was real. After they both came out of the vision, the first man walked away by himself weeping and questioning God about the encounter. The pastor felt led of the Lord to tell the man that he had seen him and his encounter, describing in perfect detail what Jesus had shown him. When the man heard the pastor explain in vivid detail the encounter, he knew that God had answered his thoughts and confirmed to him that his visitation was real.

Likewise, many of our team/tour members had similar experiences while at Bethel. Several of them were actually taken to Heaven together, where Jesus instructed three people at once. When a team member told me that she went to Heaven with other people who were present, I immediately separated them and interviewed them each separately. Sure enough, they had each been together and been told the exact same things by Jesus.

I also had an encounter with Jesus on that day. I won't go into detail here, but the one thing Jesus told me was that I was also to go to some of the Muslim nations. Because of our blessing Israel and the sons of Isaac, we were now permitted to have an effectual door with the sons of Ishmael. Within less than a month we were in Dubai and Qatar in large packed-out meetings—we were able to meet with government officials as well.

GALILEE: THE MIRACLE PORTAL

Another spiritual gateway is in the Galilee area in northern Israel. There is an unusual open Heaven portal for healings, miracles, and signs and wonders, as well as salvations. Most of Jesus's miracles were done in the Galilee area. Elijah also performed many of his miracles near Galilee, including calling fire down from Heaven at nearby Mt. Carmel. On our last trip to the Galilee area, people started to receive gold teeth, and an Arab young man who just happened to be there saw the miracles and immediately ran up to be saved and filled with the Holy Spirit.

Amazingly, we began to see gold teeth appear in people's mouths in 1999 in Tel Aviv among a meeting of Jews. What was amazing is that this was just over 50 years since Israel became a nation in 1948. The Nazis had pulled out the gold teeth of many Jews during World War II and also stole large amounts of the Jews' money and gold. The Nazis sent the loot to Swiss banks. When the gold teeth began to appear, I spoke about Jubilee, which happens every 50 years, when God restores what was lost, and the people began to understand. That same month, Swiss banks confessed to having gold that the Nazis took from the Jews, and that they were beginning the process to allocate some of this gold and money to descendants of Jews killed and robbed.

This is a sign that God is restoring not only teeth and finances but also the Messiah to Jewish people once again in the last days. What I have noticed is that, even if God does not tell you the significance or meaning of a miracle, it does not mean it is not God—look for the fruit. Often the Greek mindset in the western church seeks "wisdom," and the Jews seek a sign. Well, those signs were enough to lead them to the Messiah.

At another time, we ministered on the shores of Galilee at a New Age fair attended by over 20,000 Israeli youth who were involved heavily in the occult, drugs, and even satanism. We saw people receiving their own Jewish Messiah left and right as the power of God through the prophetic and healing mantle flowed with such ease there. Great grace was upon us all because there is an open Heaven portal there for demonstrations of power and love for the lost. Since then, we have noticed that whatever we have seen or experienced in seed form in Israel will start to be multiplied many times over in other nations we may visit.

We speak much about redigging the wells of revival in places in the western world that once had a revival. How about revisiting some of the deepest ancient wells that are still open today in Israel—and then taking that glory back to our cities and nations?

GOD'S DESIRE FOR JERUSALEM

On one of my visits to Jerusalem, I began to seek the Lord concerning the city itself. I asked the Lord what His plans were for the city in the near future. Many people have differing views concerning God's timetable for the city, so I wanted to hear from the Lord. The Lord began to speak to me of revival coming to the Holy City.

What a place to have revival! We often speak about revival returning to the United States, England, and other countries that once experienced a move of God, but what better place for a revival than Israel? After all, the very first Christian revival took place there.

The Lord showed me that in the same way people fly into cities that are currently spiritual centers of revival in various parts of the world, people from all nations (the saved and the unsaved alike) will come to Jerusalem in the days ahead, because of the glory of the Lord that is evident there.

What the Lord showed me is not to be confused with the New Jerusalem of which the Scriptures speak. He was speaking of the modern city of Jerusalem:

> *For thus says the Lord of hosts: "Just as I deter-*
> *mined to punish you when your fathers provoked*
> *Me to wrath," says the Lord of hosts, "and I would*

not relent, so again in these days I am determined
to do good to Jerusalem and to the house of Judah"
(Zechariah 8:14-15).

God is once again ready to bless the ancient city of Jerusalem. In fact, He's already doing it. I have never sensed the presence of God's glory as I do when I am in Jerusalem. When we were in the Upper Room this last time, my wife and I led a young Korean man to the Lord. He, like many others, had come to Israel searching for God.

This confirms God's promise:

> *Thus says the Lord of hosts: "Peoples shall yet come,*
> *inhabitants of many cities; the inhabitants of one*
> *city shall go to another, saying, 'Let us continue to*
> *go and pray before the Lord, and seek the Lord of*
> *hosts. I myself will go also.' Yes, many peoples and*
> *strong nations shall come to seek the Lord of hosts*
> *in Jerusalem, and to pray before the Lord." Thus*
> *says the Lord of hosts: "In those days ten men from*
> *every language of the nations shall grasp the sleeve*
> *of a Jewish man, saying, 'Let us go with you, for*
> *we have heard that God is with you'"* (Zechariah
> 8:20-23).

We have yet to see this promise come to pass in the city of Jerusalem, but it will happen. This is why it is so important to pray for Israel and for the city of Jerusalem in particular.

This does not mean that Jerusalem will always be popular, but there is something unique about the city that sets it apart from all others. After all, it is to Jerusalem that the Lord Himself will one day return (see Zech. 14:3-4).

THE EDEN OF GOD

The Garden of Eden sets the precedent as a geographical location where Heaven and earth were supernaturally linked. Adam and Eve walked in the Garden of Eden while simultaneously walking with God. Eden was a portal or point of entry into the supernatural world. It was like an embassy of Heaven located on the earth, a place where, once you set foot in it, you were both in heavenly realms and on the earth walking and talking with God in the cool of the day.

The fact that God kicked Adam and Eve out of the Garden and placed an angel with a sword to guard it reveals that it was a real location that stayed open even after they sinned. Also, Genesis 2:8 says that God placed man in the Garden after He created him, so Eden may have been a hidden place that man could not have found on his own; perhaps it is still hidden. Could there still be a physical Garden of Eden located on the earth but hidden by a thin veil that divides the natural from the supernatural? Could the same angel be guarding it for those to whom God grants access, those who have knowledge of the glory?

Another explanation can be that the physical location of Eden, the closest portal between Heaven and earth, still exists today but is veiled from most people's understanding except through revelation because of recent world events that would blind the casual observer from seeing its true location. The Garden of Eden was most likely located where Jerusalem is today.

Here are some of the reasons: Jerusalem is in the center of the area where the four rivers coming out of Eden had their headwaters. The fountain of one of the rivers, Gihon, is still in

Jerusalem today. The tree of life was in the Garden of Eden. According to Ezekiel and Zechariah, the river with the tree of life will flow out from Jerusalem and then down into the Dead Sea as well as the Mediterranean Sea.

Yet another reason is that in Ezekiel 28:13-14 it connects the Garden of Eden with God's holy mountain. It says about lucifer, "You were in Eden, the garden of God...you were on the holy mountain of God." God repeatedly calls Jerusalem *"My holy mountain,"* and *"the navel of the earth"* in Ezekiel 38:12 (MSG). It is the connecting point between Heaven and earth.

Even Abraham offered up Isaac in this place on Mount Moriah, as God told him not to sacrifice him anywhere else except "on one of the mountains I will tell you about." Abraham most likely saw a glimpse of the future death and resurrection of the Messiah as he reasoned that God could raise the dead, and figuratively speaking, he did receive Isaac back (see Heb. 11:19). He most likely saw a glimpse of the Messiah as John 8:56 says, *"Your Father Abraham rejoiced at the thought of seeing My day, and he saw it and was glad."*

As God is a God of covenant and restoration, He has been in the process of repeatedly making the same covenant with man from the beginning to restore what was lost. As Abraham offered Isaac in Jerusalem and saw a glimpse of the Messiah's ultimate sacrifice that would occur there, and as Solomon built the temple again on the same spot on Mount Moriah in Jerusalem and sacrificed there too with the glory reappearing, the Garden of Eden was most likely where God killed the first sacrifice that provided the skin that covered Adam and Eve's nakedness after the fall, foreshadowing the method and place of man's ultimate redemption. The Messiah is truly *"the Lamb slain from the foundation of the world"* (Rev 13:8).

If blood sacrifice was God's method of reconnecting us back into relation with Him and the supernatural, then the spot where the first and final blood sacrifice occurred that reopened the portal from Heaven to earth and man to God in Jerusalem must be at least part of the reason that there is such a portal of God's glory still residing in Jerusalem.

Chapter 5

SEASONAL PORTALS

When we sync with Heaven, things happen on earth as they are in Heaven. One of the ways to be in sync with Heaven is to do things when Heaven does them. And one of the ways we do this is through worshiping God at His "appointed times." We should spend time with God every day, but there are certain times in the year God asks us to set aside time with Him and He promises "special" blessings that would not come any other way. These appointed times are the feasts of God. The three major ones are Passover, Pentecost, and the fall feasts that lead into the Feast of Tabernacles.

When we celebrate these feasts at the appointed times that God set up, we see amazing heavenly abundance come in multiple ways. Imagine if after Jesus's death they stopped celebrating Pentecost and never met in that Upper Room again. That year, right after Jesus had been crucified and resurrected, the Holy Spirit showed up and filled everyone with the baptism of the Holy Spirit.

In Heaven there are things that occur at appointed times. Heaven is the realm of eternity. God mentioned that these feasts were to be celebrated eternally. When we tap into the exact timing of what is occurring in Heaven, a major heavenly download occurs, which I like to call seasonal portals.

Many people have heard about geographical portals or places where God's glory and presence reside, but there are also "seasonal" portals or appointed times that the Bible clearly says God has set on the calendar, waiting for us to meet with Him in a special way. It's like a birthday. You love your spouse or child every day, but once a year there is a special celebration of that loved one. These feats are open invitations from God for a holy rendezvous with Him.

PASSOVER

For years, without ever having any revelation on the feasts, I have always noticed the glory, power, blessing, and harvest of souls to be greater when I am doing meetings during Passover than at any other time during the year. We now purposefully do many of our conferences and outreaches during these times, and we always see "over the top" levels of God's glory, miracles, signs and wonders, salvations, revelation, and provision.

We started our Paris in the Glory Crusades in Paris, France, during Passover of 2001. God blessed each conference so much that we began holding a crusade every three months in a large arena that Benny Hinn and Morris Cerullo would rent when they came to that nation. We would see Muslims, Jews, Europeans, and others, who would otherwise never be so open to the gospel, run to be saved. There always seemed to be an unusual grace for this sudden, unexpected openness to the gospel. The meetings, along with the miracles, were so amazing that most people only hear about them in third-world countries.

We continue to do these meetings in Sedona, Arizona, and all over the U.S., with the greatest open Heaven and glory encounters that many who have come can attest to. At our last conference in Sedona during Passover, people flew in from the four corners of the U.S., the Caribbean, Italy, Austria, and Hungary, and experienced creative miracles, the manifestation of the fragrance of the Lord, as well as many other miracles.

Steve Swanson, who was leading worship one day, began to weep as he testified that he was not touching any of the instruments or keyboards. Everyone saw him shaking his head as the angels began singing during the message. Also, we saw miracles, such as thyroid problems and cancers healed, deaf ears open, instant weight loss miracles, cataracts disappear, and many other signs and wonders too numerous to list. During one of the meetings, the Lord told us not to take an offering because all the expenses would be taken care of. A few minutes later, as I was leaving the meeting, a businessman came up to me and told us God asked him to pay all the expenses of the conference, which he did. Everything seems to flow effortlessly when we hit the seasonal portal.

Jesus's Last Supper with His disciples was none other than the Passover meal during the Feast of Passover. If Jesus and the apostles celebrated Passover, then to Jesus it must be important. In fact, Jesus renewed the covenant of blood sacrifice with us to reopen the ancient pathway with His own blood. That is why both Jewish and Gentile believers continued to celebrate Passover for many years after His death—it was not only connected with Israel escaping from Egypt but with Jesus becoming our Passover Lamb.

We see this begin to change hundreds of years later after Jerusalem had already been destroyed by the Romans due to a Jewish rebellion in A.D. 66 (which is well documented in world history books) that led to its destruction by A.D. 70. Jesus prophesied this would occur in Matthew 24:2.

Due to this, by A.D. 325, during the time of Constantine, there was still much anti-Israel sentiment as Rome was now the new headquarters of much of the church for both Jewish and Gentile believers. Constantine began to close up this ancient pathway by abolishing the celebration of Passover and other biblical feasts at the biblical times and replacing them with other hybrid forms. For instance, Passover became a mixture of Jesus's death and resurrection and a pagan celebration—celebrated on a different day and with a different name. Constantine called it Easter, after Ishtar, who was the goddess of fertility and whom many in pagan Rome still worshiped.[22]

By doing this, Constantine thought he could please the many new believers in Jesus but still mix in pagan practices on pagan holidays to also please the pagans. Traditions like Easter egg hunts originated from such pagan practices. "There is no indication of the observance of the Easter festival in the New Testament, or in the writings of the apostolic Fathers.... The first Christians [the original true church]...continued to observe the Jewish [that is, God's] festivals, though in a new spirit, as commemorations of events which those festivals had foreshadowed. Thus the Passover, with a new conception added to it, of Christ, as the true Paschal Lamb and the first fruits from the dead, continued to be observed."[23]

How could the church have moved in such power and unity at its inception in Israel, spread all over the Roman Empire with miracles and resurrections, and yet eventually be degraded to a form of religion denying the power?

The feasts are not so much rules today to attain any sense of holiness as they are God's perspective and revelation from Heaven so that things on earth may be aligned with what goes on in Heaven. God promised to visit His people during specific seasons of time known as the feasts. And if God opened the heavens in both the Old and New Testament during these seasons, why would the same God of yesterday, today, and forever not show up in the same and even greater extraordinary ways again today during these seasons—these divine appointments with God when we purposefully take the time out to worship Him and feast on Him?

The fact that God even restores, for example, the Feast of Tabernacles (see Zechariah 14 about its restoration in the last days upon His return to earth with the Messiah now as the reason for the season) points to the fact that these are seasons in God where we can expect God to visit us according to His Word. Jesus even told them to wait for the promises to be fulfilled after His departure in certain *kairos* seasons of time (see Luke 24:49; Acts 1:4).

WHEN THE ANCIENT PATHS CLOSED

The following statement was dictated at the Council of Nicaea in A.D. 325, and was sent out to all the churches:

> From the letter of the Emperor [Constantine] to all those not present at the Council.[24] When the

question relative to the sacred festivals of Easter arose, it was universally thought that it would be convenient that all should keep the feast on one day; for what could be more desirable than to see this festival, through which we receive the hope of immortality, celebrated by all with one accord and in the same manner? It was declared to be particularly unworthy for this, the holiest of festivals, to follow the custom [the calculation] of the Jews, who had soiled their hands with the most fearful of crimes, and whose minds were blinded. In rejecting their custom, we may transmit to our descendants the legitimate mode of celebrating Easter; which we have observed from the time of the Savior's Passion to the present day [according to the day of the week]. We ought not, therefore, to have anything in common with the Jews, for the Savior has shown us another way; our worship follows a more legitimate and more convenient course (the order of the days of the week); and consequently, in unanimously adopting this mode, we desire, dearest brethren, to separate ourselves from the detestable company of the Jew, for it is truly shameful for us to hear them boast that without their direction we could not keep this feast. How can they be in the right, they who, after the death of the Savior, have no longer been led by reason but by wild violence, as their delusion may urge them? They do not possess the truth in this Easter question, for, in their blindness and repugnance to all improvements, they frequently celebrate two Passovers in the same year.

We could not imitate those who are openly in error. How, then, can we follow these Jews, who are most certainly blinded by error? For to celebrate a Passover twice in one year is totally inadmissible. But even if this were not so, it would still be your duty not to tarnish your soul by communications with such wicked people [the Jews].... You should consider not only that the number of churches in these provinces make a majority, but also that it is right to demand what our reason approves, and that we should have nothing in common with the Jews.[25]

Obviously, Constantine did not understand the ancient paths enough to know that they did not celebrate two Passovers, but simply the different biblical feasts and celebrations of the Lord.

The problem with Easter and Ishtar is that ancient worshipers of Ishtar, the goddess of fertility, would have sexual orgies in the name of Ishtar. The Ishtar Festivals were symbolical of Ishtar as the goddess of love or generation.

As the daughter of Sin, the moon god, she was the Mother Goddess who presided over child birth, and women, in her honor, sacrificed their virginity on the feast day or became temple prostitutes, their earnings being a source of revenue for the temple priests and servants. We learn about these temple prostitutes from *The Interpreter's Dictionary of The Bible*: "Astarte of Phoenicia was the offshoot of Ishtar of Assyria. To the Hebrews, this abomination was known as Ashtoreth/Ashtoroth."[26]

From *Collier's Encyclopedia* we read: "Ashtaroth [Æ-terath] the plural of the Hebrew 'Ashto-reth,' the Phoenician-Canaanite goddess Astarte, deity of fertility, reproduction, and war."[27]

No wonder the true believers did not agree with Constantine on changing the Passover date set by God to resemble a pagan name and holiday and trying to mix the resurrection of Jesus into it.

That is how colored Easter Eggs got lumped together with the celebration of Easter, even in churches in many western nations today—those most influenced by the Roman Empire. Did you know that dyed Easter eggs also figured in the ancient Babylonian mystery rites, just as they do in Easter observance today? Yes, these are pagan too.

It is recorded that the ancient Druids bore an egg as the sacred emblem of their idolatrous order.[28] Eggs were sacred to many ancient civilizations and formed an integral part of the religious ceremonies in Egypt and in the Orient. According to James Bonwick:

> Eggs were hung up in the Egyptian temples. Bunsen calls attention to the mundane egg, the emblem of generative life, proceeding from the mouth of the great god of Egypt. The mystic egg of Babylon, hatching the Venus Ishtar, fell from heaven to the Euphrates. Dyed eggs were sacred Easter offerings in Egypt, as they are still in China and Europe. Easter, or spring, was the season of birth, terrestrial and celestial.[29]

There is not a word of it in the New Testament. Certainly Christ did not start it, and the apostles and early Christians did none of it.

It appears that celebrating Passover was actually encouraged to be kept, but to be done in the newness of what Jesus did for us. In First Corinthians 5:7-8, Paul tells the Corinthians: *"Christ, our Passover, was sacrificed for us. Therefore let us keep the feast, not with old leaven...but with the unleavened bread of sincerity and truth."* And in the 11th chapter he gives the directions regarding this ordinance. Jesus fulfills the feast, not abolishes it, and the glory of this seasonal portal can be opened as it was in the early church and even the apostles continued it.

Some misunderstand First Corinthians 11:26, which says, *"As often as you eat this bread and drink this cup,"* by interpreting it as "take it as often as you wish." But it does not necessary say that. It says "as often" as you observe it "you proclaim the Lord's death till He comes." Even Jesus commanded, *"This do, as often as you drink it, in remembrance of Me"* (1 Cor. 11:25). We do it in remembrance of the Lord's death—a memorial of His death.

No wonder we no longer have the same open Heaven portal that we could have had. If we are going to celebrate Passover and Pentecost, for example, as many do in the church today, why should we change the date that God has set to visit us, and why should we name it after a pagan goddess? Somehow we have diluted the power of God in doing this. Have you ever wondered how we got the Easter eggs, and how the name Easter came about? Or why we celebrate Easter instead of Passover as Jesus and the disciples did during the Last Supper? How can we allow this mixture, adding colored eggs and bunnies and thereby changing the seasonal portal? Bunnies are often associated with sexuality and fertility and have been used by pagan religions for centuries.

It's one thing not to celebrate God's feasts because of a lack of revelation, but it's quite another to mix God's feasts with paganism. When we line up with God's seasonal, appointed times, great blessing from Heaven is the result. We will begin to walk into the fullness of all that the Jewish apostles and prophets possessed as we step back into the ancient paths.[1]

Here are a few excerpts from one of the most recognized historians of the early church regarding the apostles like Phillip, John, and other saints and how they regarded this seasonal portal. Eusebius, historian of the early centuries of the church, speaks of the true Christians observing Passover on the 14th of Nisan, first month of the Sacred Calendar.

> A question of no small importance arose at that time. For the parishes of all Asia, as from an older tradition, held that the fourteenth day of the moon, on which day the Jews were commanded to sacrifice the lamb, should be observed as the feast of the Savior's Passover...the bishops of Asia, led by Polycrates, decided to hold to the old custom handed down to them. He himself, in a letter which he addressed to Victor and the church of Rome, set forth in the following words the tradition which had come down to him:
>
> We observe the exact day; neither adding, nor taking away. For in Asia also great lights have fallen asleep, which shall rise again on the day of the Lord's coming, when He shall come with glory from Heaven,

---

1 I know a prophet named Bob Jones. Every year on Yom Kippur, another ancient seasonal portal and symbolically the holiest day of the year, God gives him some of his most profound prophetic words and experiences for our nation. Let's not get religious about it, but let's tap into the portal of these ancient seasonal paths that are still available today to all who are covered in the blood of the Lamb.

and shall seek out all the saints. Among these are Philip, one of the twelve apostles...and, moreover, John, who was both a witness and a teacher, who reclined upon the bosom of the Lord...and Polycarp in Smyrna, who was a bishop and martyr; and Thraseas, bishop and martyr from Eumenia...the bishop and martyr Sagaris...the blessed Papirius, or Melito.... All these observed the fourteenth day of the Passover according to the Gospel, deviating in no respect, but following the rule of faith.[30]

PENTECOST (FEAST OF WEEKS)

When the early church obeyed Jesus's command to wait in the Upper Room, many do not realize that they waited in the Upper Room during the Feast of Weeks (or Pentecost), a feast that had been celebrated by Israel for centuries (see Exod. 34:21-23; Lev. 23:15-22; Deut. 16:9-12,16; 2 Chron. 8:13; Ezek. 1:13). This was one of the feasts that God told Moses and the Israelites to celebrate. For Israel, the Feast of Weeks is all about celebrating the giving of the law and the Ten Commandments.

This is part of reactivating the mantle that Moses walked in; but now it is for all believers. When the disciples obeyed and waited on the Lord during that specific feast, praising and worshiping Him, the heavens opened and the power of God was released. All believers went out from there full of the Holy Spirit, doing healings, miracles, signs, and deliverances, as boldness came upon them.

This power at Pentecost was not released in the years before because they did not yet have access into the supernatural that came through the blood sacrifice. The blood of Jesus became the first doorway into the supernatural; now all believers could experience the supernatural as Moses once had. Now believers moved powerfully in both the Word and the Spirit.

When Peter preached that day, he did not quote from the New Testament or the Book of Acts, for they had not yet been written. He and all the believers read from the ancient Hebrew Scriptures, now often referred to as the Old Testament. When they reread and preached these Scriptures with revelation, as the blood of Jesus provided access to the supernatural, the same power and glory that Moses and Elijah experienced was released.

The New Testament believers were told to study to show themselves approved (see 2 Tim. 2:15). The Books of Matthew, Mark, Luke, and John, and the books written by Paul were still in the making as at that time, especially Paul's writings, which were called letters. In the letter to Timothy he was not telling Timothy to keep reading his own letters over and over to himself, but he was referring to the Hebrew Scriptures that we call the Old Testament. The only book they had to study was the Old Testament, but the Holy Spirit falling on the Word caused the power of the ancient glories to be reawakened into new glory. Jesus basically came to restore the spirit of what God was saying all along through the Scriptures and to redirect it in the right way.

In fact, most of the New Testament totally interacts with the Old, as it is a fulfillment of the ancient Hebrew Scriptures. Jesus read from the Book of Isaiah and told the people that what He read about being "the One" was fulfilled in their hearing. Jesus said that if they really believed in the book of Moses then they would believe in Him. Peter said, "This is that," which was prophesied referring to the book of Joel. When we say everything has to be backed up by the Word of God, that was the exact concept the people of Israel used. Jesus had to line up with the word of God and the Messiah that was prophesied in their Scriptures to be coming.

People believed in Jesus and His message because it lined up with the Word of God, the Hebrew Scriptures, the only Scriptures that existed in the time of Jesus.

FEAST OF TABERNACLES

The Feast of Tabernacles is also a very powerful seasonal portal that many are starting to realize once again. It is so powerful that when Messiah the King returns to rule and reign in Jerusalem, Zechariah 14:16 says He will restore this feast. This is another ancient pathway to the glory of God.

> *And it shall come to pass that everyone who is left of all the nations which came against Jerusalem shall go up from year to year to worship the King, the Lord of hosts, and to keep the Feast of Tabernacles* (Zechariah 14:16).

The Israelites celebrated this feast, as did the early church (including Gentile believers), for the first few hundred years. If Jesus is going to restore the feasts that have been forgotten, including the Feast of Tabernacles, why not tap into this seasonal portal and the future blessings it releases now? Many think it is only a Jewish feast; but, according Zechariah, it is a feast for all nations.

> *And it shall be that whichever of the families of the earth do not come up to Jerusalem to worship the*

> *King, the Lord of hosts, on them there will be no*
> *rain* (Zechariah 14:17).

God is promising to open the heavens and pour out rain if we will simply honor Him during this exact time. How each person, group, or church celebrates Him is really not the point, but taking the time to honor God during Tabernacles is a major key. Rain is symbolic of both spiritual and material blessings.

God will open the heavens and pour out rain on people and nations who will walk into this seasonal portal both now and in the future. This feast is a major seasonal portal, and Jerusalem itself is a physical portal. When you combine a geographical portal with a seasonal portal (as will occur when the King returns to Jerusalem), the result is Heaven on earth. Though to many it may now appear optional to celebrate these feasts—as our salvation is not dependent on these ancient pathways or feasts but on the sacrifice Jesus paid on the cross, it does allow us to tap into a greater glory. And we now know that it will be mandatory if we want His "rain" at His return (see Zech. 14:17-18).

God is so serious about His invitation that when the King returns, serious consequences will occur for those who choose not to respond to His invitation to the holy party. Zechariah again says,

> *If the family of Egypt will not come up and enter*
> *in, they shall have no rain; they shall receive the*
> *plague with which the Lord strikes the nations who*
> *do not come up to keep the Feast of Tabernacles*
> (Zechariah 14:18).

Even Arab nations will be not only invited, but required to enter into this time of open Heaven encounters during the feast in Jerusalem. In fact, Zechariah lists plagues that will come if these nations choose to pass on the invitation. This again proves that the feast is not a Jewish feast but a feast for all nations who will worship Jesus, the Jewish Messiah, as the King of the earth.

The other side to this is the physical portal. When the Gentile nations come to Jerusalem, they are admitting that God has chosen Jerusalem and Israel as the biggest portal on the earth for His glory. I believe that when Arab believers begin to celebrate Jesus purposely during these seasonal portals—even in their own nations right now—great "rain," revival, and harvest will erupt like never before in the Arab nations and all nations of the world.

God will also use the Arab believers to make the Jews jealous for their Messiah, for they will see Arab believers rejoicing before God and God manifesting His power and glory among them. The Jews will wonder why God is showing up among the Gentiles. They will find their answer in the access all believers have been granted through the blood sacrifice of Jesus.

SHABBAT (THE LORD'S DAY)

There remaineth therefore a rest to the people of God. For he that is entered into his rest, he also hath ceased from his own works, as God did from his. Let us labour therefore to enter into that rest, lest any man fall after the same example of unbelief (Hebrews 4:9-12 KJV).

A weekly heavenly seasonal portal can occur also. God designed humans to rest once a week. It is even written in the Ten Commandments. When you take one day a week to rest from your usual income-earning labors and spend time with God, read His Word, enjoy His creation, and spend quality time with family, you tap into a supernatural dimension of rest you would not otherwise have experienced.

Biblical Shabbat, observed from Friday night sundown until Saturday night sundown, is practiced even today in Israel and in Jewish families around the world. Christians often take Sundays off. But I've noticed that rushing to church sometimes twice that day is not always a rest. I still enjoy taking my Friday night to Saturday off. It makes a huge difference in my week. Often I am speaking on the weekends, so I will do a Friday night service then sleep in and enjoy deep rest and intimacy with the Lord, often going for a walk in nature. As I do, fresh creative ideas from Heaven will just flow.

When I don't get that one day off, I can feel a huge difference. When I rest that day I am more clear minded and my body is relaxed; I feel happier. I am able to put all the business of life on pause, redirect my life, and reevaluate my destiny to make sure it's on the right track. Often I get fresh direction and visions that day.

The Bible clearly says the feasts are God's feasts (see Lev. 23:2), but Exodus says that the Sabbath was made for rest (see Exod. 31:15). It was not necessarily a day to burn ourselves out for God, but to rest and be refreshed in God: *"The Sabbath was made for man, and not man for the Sabbath"* (Mark 2:27).

Jesus Himself never spoke against the Sabbath. He only shed light on the fact that the Sabbath was made for humans, even affirming it. He only corrected the Pharisees when they tried to add a legalistic spirit by forbidding someone to help another person or even an animal on the Sabbath.

That being said, there is something of a greater open Heaven portal for rest, healing, and refreshing that occurs between Friday night and Saturday night. You can take that 24-hour period and spend time soaking in the presence of God as your mind, body, and spirit rests and gets refreshed in Him. Also, when you do minister during that time, it has been my experience that you can expect a greater flow of the miraculous. The early church observed the Sabbath and spent time with God on that day. Of course, all of Israel basically shut down for that day, including all businesses, so this made it pretty easy to take that day off with God.

Also, a recent publication in alternative medicine has suggested that resting from Friday sundown to Saturday sundown promotes optimal rejuvenation of the cells in your body due to the effect that the moon cycles have on the earth during that 24 hour period each week.[31] Either way, the Bible says that God rested on the seventh day as an example for man to follow even before it was ever a command.

If you have a full-time job, it is a blessing to have at least one day off to rest, pray, and hang out with family and friends to recuperate, otherwise one starts to feel like a rat in a rat race or a slave. In Deuteronomy, the commandment to "observe" the Sabbath day is tied to the experience of a people newly released from bondage. You get to have a day off, not so much a command to restrict you but to free you from the everyday routine. Slaves cannot take a day off; free people can. When they stop work every seventh day, the people will remember that the Lord brought them out of slavery, and they will see to it that no one within their own dominion, not even animals, will work without respite.

Sabbath rest is a recurring testimony against the drudgery of slavery. Whatever you believe about it, most doctors and nutritionists today will tell you that resting at least one day, especially when sick, is the quickest way to recovery and energy. Also, on the flip side, people who work and never take a day to rest after a while noticeably have more of a tendency to get sick, be irritable, experience emotional symptoms like depression, and simply not be as happy as those who have a free day to rest and enjoy God and family.

The Bible does not specifically command us to go to church on Sunday, though there is nothing wrong with it; many have that day off, and it is now a common practice. The only reason some believers biblically gathered on the first day of the week, Sunday, was because tithes, alms giving, and business of any kind could not be conducted on the Sabbath, as the entire nation of Israel shut down to worship God that day. That does not mean that believers did not take the Sabbath to rest, be with family, and worship God as He opened the heavens.

By the time of Constantine, and enforced more cruelly by his later successor as emperor, Theodosius, it was forbidden, especially for Jewish and Gentile believers, to have church on Saturday and to celebrate other feasts; they were threatened by death and excommunication by Gentile believers for doing so. Even *The Catholic Encyclopedia* acknowledged that the Roman and Orthodox Churches got the emperors to persecute those who did not accept what became beliefs of mainstream "Christianity":

> When Constantine had taken upon himself the office of lay bishop, *episcopus externus,* and put

the secular arm at the service of the church, the laws against heretics became more and more rigorous. Under the purely ecclesiastical discipline no temporal punishment could be inflicted on the obstinate heretic, except the damage which might arise to his personal dignity through being deprived of all intercourse with his former brethren. But under the Christian emperors rigorous measures were enforced against the goods and persons of heretics. From the time of Constantine to Theodosius…Theodosius is said to be the first who pronounced heresy a capital crime; this law was passed in 382.[32]

Edicts of Theodosius against the heretics, A.D. 380-394…Theodosius…decreed that…by the death of the offender; and the same capital punishment was inflicted on the Audians, or Quartodecimans, who should dare to perpetrate the atrocious crime of celebrating on an improper day the festival…. The theory of persecution was established by Theodosius, whose justice and piety have been applauded by the saints.[33]

Again, the reason was the spirit of anti-Semitism in the government that prejudiced Gentile believers against their Jewish brothers in the Lord due to the last war with Israel. To this day, there has been this sort of separation, but the Bible says that He will restore one new man from both Jews and Gentiles to minister and worship together (see Eph. 2:14-15).

Satan knows that there is a seasonal portal during these times, and so he has used the religious spirit to shut it down by accusing people who worship God on those days of having a "religious spirit" themselves: *"Let no one judge you in food or in drink, or regarding a festival or a new moon or Sabbaths"* (Col. 2:16). This verse also indicates that believers should not let anyone judge them when they celebrate the ancient open Heaven feast times in their proper season.

That does not mean we should not go to church on Sunday. On the contrary, Sunday is already a day off of work, and at this point in history, it is a very convenient time to meet with other believers who also have the day off. On the same note, it is an important thing to repent of the anti-Semitism spirit that the early Gentile church leaders had when they officially established Sunday as the "day of the Lord," thus robbing many of the revelation of the feasts and the true Sabbath rest day. Let us not forsake the gathering of ourselves together which is often on Sunday—even though it is not the Sabbath. You can also choose to take from Friday night until Saturday night to worship God, sleep in, go for a walk in His creation, read the Word, and soak in His presence with family, so that by the time you get to church on Sunday you will be full of God's glory.

That being said, every day should be a day of the Lord as we expect God to visit us daily, declaring,

> *[His mercies] are new every morning...* (Lamentations 3:23).

And,

> *This is the day the Lord has made; we will rejoice and be glad in it* (Psalm 118:24).

FIRST FRUITS (ROSH CHODESH)

Like Shabbat is weekly, First Fruits is a monthly pause to seek the Lord, worship together with His people, receive from the prophetic, and give to God. What we do during that first day of the month will determine the blessing of the next 30 days. You are in essence giving God the first fruit or the first day of that month, asking Him to bless the rest. Once I tapped into this revelation, the favor and breakthroughs have been mind-boggling. I really think the enemy has kept away much of the needed revelation in the Word of God to keep us from reaching our highest potential in God and in life in general. He tries to make us think that these things are no longer for us today, when actually we are invited to the same blessings of Abraham as the Jews have as we are grafted in through Jesus our Jewish Messiah. We are the adopted kids; we get to show up to the celebrations too!

This monthly cycle falls on the new moon of each month. A good Hebrew calendar will help you know what day is the first day of first fruits each month from sundown to sundown (see Num. 28:11-15; Ps. 81:3-4; 1 Sam. 20: 5, 18; 2 Kings 4:23; Isa. 66:23). I also recommend a great book on this subject, *A Time to Advance*, by Chuck Pierce with Robert and Linda Heidler.

Chapter 6

HEAVEN'S GLORY

VISITING HEAVEN

I was in Bethel, Israel, leading a tour some time ago. I knew that Bethel was the place where Jacob laid down to sleep one night, resting his head on a rock, when he had a visitation from God. While he slept, he dreamed that there was a staircase descending from Heaven to the earth, and he saw angels ascending and descending on it. Bethel is the place in the Bible where Jacob said, *"How awesome is this place! This is none other than the house of God; this is **the gate of heaven**"* (Gen. 28:17 NIV). I figured that if we soaked and prayed in a place the Bible called a "gate of Heaven," then it would be much easier to access the heavenly realm.

We drove up to the site (in a bulletproof bus, since we had to pass Ramallah to get there), but no one really knew exactly where in Bethel to go. So the driver dropped us off at a spot where settlers were living near a big water tower. We walked about half a mile and found the perfect location—a big round slab of concrete and rocks all around.

I had our worship leader play his guitar for the entire hour or so we were there, while our team laid down on the slab. Many of us even found a rock to lay our head, just as Jacob had done thousands of years before us. Then, as the music played, I just closed my eyes and let the Holy Spirit take me as I cleared my mind of any of my own thoughts. Within a few minutes, my spiritual eyes opened.

On one side I could see our team on the floor; but then the scene changed, and it was as if I walked through an invisible wall. Suddenly, I was in Heaven at the crystal sea. As I looked across the sea, there stood Jesus. I was suddenly right in front of Him. His eyes were like fire, yet at the same time pure love was pouring out of Him. He looked at me and said these words: "Thank you for touching Isaac, My people. Now would you also reach out to Ishmael?"

I responded almost immediately, saying, "Yes, of course, my Lord."

Then He proceeded to ask me a second question: "Would you please also organize a conference for Me in Jerusalem?" I was surprised because I did not live in Israel. I thought to myself, "Who am I to organize a conference in Jerusalem?" But, being in the amazing glory of the moment, it was almost impossible to say anything else but, "Yes, Lord," which I did.

About two days after we had the Bethel experience, we ended our stay at the Dead Sea. A fellow minister asked me if I would organize a conference in Jerusalem to reach out and bless Jewish people after they do a conference in Bethlehem to reach the Arabs and feed the poor. I told him that normally I would have said no, but because Jesus had directly asked me two days before in Bethel to reach out to Ishmael, I said yes.

The second confirmation of my Bethel experience was that, immediately after I got home, I was invited for the first time to Muslim nations to share the gospel. Within just a few weeks of Jesus asking me to reach Ishmael, I was in Kuwait seeing salvations and miracles among the people there. Then God opened up Dubai, Abu Dhabi, Qatar, Bahrain, and Indonesia, where thousands were saved, healed, and delivered.

I could have easily dismissed the experience as a vision of my own mind and thoughts, but the proof was that shortly after, that which I saw and was told started to occur. This experience was not only unique to me, but accessing the heavenly realms can be for any believer in Christ Jesus.

HOW TO ENTER THE HEAVENLY REALMS

The easiest way to enter the heavenly realms seems to be to relax or soak to quiet music. When you relax, God can more easily speak to you. God often speaks to His people through dreams because that is the only time they are finally knocked out and their brains are more open to receive from Him, as opposed to being busy all day with errands, email, Facebook, ministry, calls, bills, etc. Our minds are one of the gateways that God uses to speak to us. It only has so much memory, like a computer chip. When the chip is full of information from the stress of our daily life, it's hard for God to download vision, direction, or heavenly experiences.

When John was on the island of Patmos, he had an easier time in this regard, as he was a prisoner on an island, unable to go anywhere, with nothing much to distract him (see Rev. 1:9). The same is also true of Paul. Spending a lot of time in jail, he had the downtime to hear and receive from the

Lord without all the daily pressures that normally accompanied him.

In my own personal times with the Lord, I usually spend the first hour praising and worshiping the Lord until His glory comes. Then I make special decrees and petitions after a time in His glory. Once in His presence and glory, I will often put on soaking music and go further into the heavenly realms, just as we did while in Bethel.

A person can lie down, put on soaking music, and rest their mind and spirit, keeping them open for the Lord to speak to them, show them a vision, or even take their spirit to Heaven. Before I go to sleep, I often tell the Lord that He is welcome to speak to me all night, which results in more dreams that are prophetic or directional. God will speak in our dreams even when uninvited, but something unusual happens when we invite Him to come.

It should go without saying that holiness is a major key to hearing God's voice, thereby entering into the heavenly realms of His glory.

LEGAL ACCESS

Believers who hold on to sin must let it go so they can more easily experience the heavenly realms. If there is any sin or offense in your heart, ask God to cleanse you and forgive you, and then repent of it. It is only those cleansed from sin who can enter into the heavenly realms. The psalmist asks the question and then gives the answer, *"Who may ascend the mountain of the Lord? Who may stand in his holy place? The one who has clean hands and a pure heart"* (Ps. 24:3 NIV).

When Jesus died on the cross, He rent the veil of the Temple in two (see Matt. 27:51), and thus made a way for us to come boldly to His throne by the blood of the Lamb. People who try to enter the supernatural realms who are not washed in His blood and who not following Jesus are actually entering illegally through a back door. But Jesus said this should not be so. To the Pharisees, Jesus said,

> *he who does not enter the sheepfold by the door, but climbs up some other way, the same is a thief and a robber. ...I am the door. If anyone enters by Me, he will be saved, and will go in and out and find pasture. The thief does not come except to steal, and to kill, and to destroy. I have come that they may have life, and that they may have it more abundantly"* (John 10:1, 9-10).

The above passage talks about people trying to climb into the sheepfold "by some other way." Many are trying to enter the supernatural realms, but they often try to get in some other way than the legal way, which comes via a direct relationship with the Messiah. Jesus's blood applied to our lives gives us legal access to go boldly to the throne of grace.

The Bible says we are to *"come boldly to the throne of grace"* (Heb. 4:16). Where is God's throne of grace located? Well, for sure there is a throne located in Heaven. God is giving us an invitation to come to Heaven where His throne is. But the Bible also says we are seated with Him in heavenly places or realms. It doesn't say we *will be* seated with Him in heavenly places; it says *"God raised us up with Christ and seated us with Him in the heavenly realms"* (Eph. 2:6 NIV). That means we have a place in Heaven *now*, not just when we die.

Revelation 4:1 says, *"There before me was a door standing open in heaven. And the voice I had first heard speaking to me like a trumpet said, 'Come up here, and I will show you what must take place after this'"* (NIV). John entered into the heavenly realm and was given major revelation about the end times— what is coming on the earth, how to prepare for it, and how it all ends. I'd say that was worth going into the heavenly realm so that the entire world of believers would know what is coming and how to prepare for it.

It's wonderful just being in the throne room of God, worshiping before Him, experiencing His presence and glory. Many times when I am in a worship service or in a meeting where I am the speaker, I will lay down on the floor during part of the worship and go up to the throne and the heavenly realm. Once there, the glory will be so much thicker, and I will often receive further instructions on what to say, what kind of miracles will take place, and what kind of angels will be coming back down with me from Heaven. Then I will get up and start the meeting.

When this takes place, many times the glory and angelic will start to break out right at the beginning with major prophetic decrees for the region, as well as miracles and healings. Often, when in that realm, I will know where one of the big angels is standing, and I will point it out to the people. People will often stand in the place that I point to, and will get knocked out by the power of God and come up totally healed or having had a heavenly encounter or visitation. Often, when there is resistance in a certain region with strongholds, or even if that resistance is in the room, I will go to the heavenly realm. When I come back down, it clobbers the demonic forces, leaving them paralyzed. Sometimes this is the best option when you sense that a breakthrough is needed. What better breakthrough than all of Heaven coming down!

While I was in Africa doing a crusade, there was a lot of resistance from witchcraft. The first night was very difficult. I determined to go into an even higher glory realm and began fasting to help get me there faster. Then, when I stood on the platform the next night, thousands of angels showed up and mass deliverances occurred even before the preaching. A demon-possessed women acting like a cat wanted to come up to the platform to scratch me—she was totally set free. Then I asked the angels to deliver the many needing deliverance, and people started to fall on the floor in droves wherever I would point to where the angels were. When they fell, we could hear thousands of people getting deliverance, screaming out and foaming at the mouth. It was so easy because the angels and Heaven did all the work as opposed to me doing deliverance. On one night in just a short time, thousands experienced deliverance.

That is the difference between the anointing and Heaven's glory. You, with your own faith and anointing, can see a few people healed and set free. But when you go up to the heavenly realm and come back down with myriads of angels and heavenly hosts, it's like the difference between a shotgun and a nuclear blast. As the days get more intense on the earth, we need to learn how to go more often into the heavenly realm and bring back greatly-needed reinforcements and greater glory.

In the story about Jacob's ladder, angels were ascending and descending the staircase to Heaven (see Gen. 28:12). That means we also can go up and down that same staircase. The difference is that when we come back down, we can often bring with us a lot more angels and a major increase in glory. This also seems to blindside the enemy and release a greater victory.

REENTERING HEAVEN

Once you have been in Heaven, either in a vision or in the spirit realm, it's much easier to get back in the next time. When you are resting in Him, just keep remembering and thinking about the last time you went up; and before you know it, you will be back in. The mind is a gateway into the spirit when you let the Lord use it. That's why we are to renew our minds according to God's Word (see Rom. 12:2). If it gets clogged up with the cares of this life, renewing our mind and thus reentering that realm becomes much harder to do.

Let's say you went to the throne of Heaven for the first time. Go back up to the throne again, as it will be the easiest port of entry if you were already there before. But this time, journey to other places in Heaven too, like the sea of glass. I love to just jump into the sea of glass in the spirit realm. I feel so refreshed and invigorated when I do this. Heaven is such an awesome place!

And remember, we don't have to wait until we die to experience it. Many believers have their ticket to Heaven now but never fully enjoy it. It's like having a ticket to Disneyland and just barely walking into the entrance of the park, never going any further to enjoy the rides. Many are satisfied they have said the sinner's prayer, but they have not gone on to experience the joy of their salvation by fully accessing all that their salvation entails, including opening up Heaven for themselves.

Chapter 7

THE COURTS OF HEAVEN

ENTERING THE COURTS OF HEAVEN

The court of Heaven is an amazing place to take care of business and see things change on the earth that otherwise may never have changed. I discovered this revelation one day when I was doing a healing meeting and many were receiving miracles. Then I noticed a crying woman sitting next to her teenage son. I asked her what the problem was. She began to explain to me that her son was going to court and most likely jail for many years due to the police having found child porn on his computer and other things he had been involved with. The boy motioned with a guilty, sad look that this was true. I brought the boy to the altar, asking him first if he wanted to be saved. He immediately said yes, and I proceeded to lead him to salvation.

Then a thought came to my mind. If things are done on earth as they are done in Heaven (see Matt. 6:10), and if God is the Judge of all the earth (see James 4:12), then there must be a courtroom in Heaven, with court cases where legal matters are dealt with. I told the boy that before he went to the earthly court, we should try to take this up with the Judge of Heaven and earth in the heavenly court, which could affect the earthly court's decisions.

We closed our eyes, and I told him that I could see us going up into the heavens where the throne is. Then I explained to him that I saw us going into the courts of Heaven. I proceeded to go into the courtroom. There I saw the Judge on His chair. There were witnesses and onlookers in the room as well, and Jesus was there. I began to address the Judge of Heaven and earth: "Your Honor," I said, and then I explained the boy's case but added that he had just repented of all his sins and received Jesus as his Lord and Savior.

Then I felt led to ask for a moment to speak with the boy and called a recess. During the recess, I went to the boy and asked him if he had a call upon his life. He told me that his mother had told him for years, since he was a little boy, that many had prophesied he had a call on his life, but he was now running from it. This opened up his life to demonic and spiritual attacks. He told me that he was so happy being saved that he wanted to give his life to the gospel, even if that meant being used in prison to witness to the other inmates—he was just happy to be saved.

I then proceeded to tell this to the Judge and Jesus, who is our Advocate (see 1 John 2:1). As we presented our case again before the Judge, I could hear the accuser of the brethren (the opposing attorney) say that the boy deserved his punishment. We countered with the argument that the blood of Jesus and repentance brings "legal" forgiveness or justification (see Rom.

5:9). Then the Judge made the final verdict. I heard Him say loud and clear, "Innocent!"

We felt such a feeling of relief. We, of course, were not sure what the actual outcome on earth would be until a few days later. During the course of the weekend, the boy kept coming to the meetings, glowing in the love and forgiveness of God. Then on the Tuesday after the weekend, he went to the courthouse. The opposing lawyer and the judge asked to speak with him briefly before the case started. They both told the boy that they had so much evidence against him that it was certain he would go to jail for years. They were both Christians and basically wanted to make sure he was right with God. They asked him if he wanted to receive the Lord first. He replied by explaining what had occurred during the weekend; how he had been gloriously saved, that he was ready to go to prison, and he hoped God would use him to reach other prisoners. They were so touched by his testimony, his attitude, the acceptance of his sin and punishment, and his salvation that the earthly judge threw the case out and he was freed to go.

Now when we pray, "Let Your will be done on earth as it is in Heaven," it takes on a whole new meaning. We can go to the courts of Heaven and take care of business there. If it gets settled in Heaven, things can change on the earth pretty fast and miraculously.

JOB'S ARGUMENTS IN THE COURTS OF HEAVEN

Job also presented arguments for his case, pleading to go straight to the Judge of Heaven and earth: *"But I desire to speak to the Almighty and to argue my case with God"* (Job 13:3

NIV). He knew that true justice would only come from the true Judge of Heaven and earth. Earthly judges don't always get it right, and court cases can go either way, no matter the evidence. Many cases are won or lost depending on how knowledgeable and experienced the lawyer is, as well as many other factors. We have the best Jewish lawyer—Jesus! And better yet, His Father is the Judge. I'd say the odds are in our favor with this Judge and this Lawyer, as long as we follow the proper protocols.

The Judge will even oftentimes deliver those who are not innocent (along with the proper protocols like repentance and being covered in the blood of the Messiah). Here is a passage that shows exactly this truth: *"He'll even deliver the guilty, who will be delivered through your innocence"* (Job 22:30 ISV).

Job goes on to say, *"Even though He kills me, I'll continue to hope in Him. **At least I'll be able to argue my case to His face!**"* (Job 13:15 ISV). Even though Job was talking about if he died because God slayed him, he still could argue his case to God. We can see throughout the Book of Job that he is actually already arguing his case and God is hearing what he is saying.

People sometimes ask me if they went one time to the Judge of Heaven with their case, is that one time enough? I always lead them to the story of the persistent widow. She kept pleading her case with the judge until he gave in and gave her what she wanted (see Luke 18:1-8). How much more will the Judge of Heaven and earth answer us? Also, there is no waiting time to get into the courtroom; the doors are always open and you don't need an appointment. Job was very persistent as he said, *"I'm not letting up—I'm standing my ground. My complaint is legitimate"* (Job 23:1-2 MSG). He went on to say, *"If only I knew* *where to find God, **I would go to His court. I would lay out my case and present my arguments"*** (Job 23:3-4 NLT).

THE ACCUSER OF THE BRETHREN

The great thing is that we have access to the Judge and can come to the court of Heaven any time we want! Jesus's blood gives us access to the throne room and to Heaven. In fact, we are presently seated with Him in heavenly places (see Eph. 2:6).

The accuser of the brethren is always there, however, ready to accuse us before the Judge. But all we have to do is show up covered in the blood of Jesus, having already repented, and present our case. If the enemy tries to bring up our past or any past sins in our life that have already been repented of and forgiven, the Judge won't allow them to be used against us as evidence; they are already under the blood and paid for. Once you understand the protocols of the courts of Heaven, get in court, and order that the enemy has to release back what has been held—you can win cases and see them manifest quickly on the earth.

What I discovered is that most Christians lose battles on the earth simply by not showing up to the courts of Heaven— they lose by default. This means that if they would simply show up to the court case and go through the protocol, they would have so many victories. When the enemy is accusing you to the Judge, it's time to take him to court. The Lord says, *"My people are destroyed for lack of knowledge"* (Hosea 4:6). We need to have not just the glory of God but also the knowledge of the glory. Knowledge of the glory can unlock the realms of Heaven.

The accuser of the brethren accuses God's people day and night: *"Then I heard a loud voice in heaven, saying, 'Now the salvation, and the power, and the kingdom of our God and the authority of His Christ have come, for the accuser of our brethren has been thrown down, he who accuses them before our God day and night'"* (Rev. 12:10 NASB).

Just like any savvy lawyer, the devil is a legalist and tries to find a loophole. The only loophole he can use, however, is if you don't show up and plead your case, or if you don't repent of anything he could use against you. You must ask God to forgive you and cleanse you with the blood of His Son Jesus before you show up in court to please your case.

There was a time I was owed a large amount of money that I did not realize was supposed to be coming to me in a far-away nation. The Holy Spirit revealed to my wife and I that the money held back was ours. I questioned the businessmen to find out if they had kept money, and sure enough, they had. They felt this substantial amount of money was theirs, since the money that we had received was sufficient, though it was only one-fourth of what we should have received. They refused to do anything at all.

The Lord pressed me to take it to the court of Heaven. At first I thought to just let it go; but the Lord taught me something that day. It's one thing to forgive someone for not being honest and not telling you the whole truth while keeping something back from you, but it's another thing to take your "adversary" to the courts of Heaven to get him to pay back what is owed you. Yes, you forgive the person or people who are involved on the earth, but spiritually you go after what was lost in the spirit realm, forcing the true spiritual enemy to release it.

So this time my wife and I fasted and prayed for 24 hours, and together we went to the courts of Heaven pleading our case. We asked God to cover us in Jesus's blood and to forgive us for any anger or unforgiveness that could be in our hearts—we fully released the people. Then we presented our case to the Judge. We heard the enemy in our minds countering with his reasoning. We countered again with the Word of God and the situation as it had occurred, covering it all in the blood. By the end of the day, we felt a total release of peace, whereas before we could sense tremendous warfare in the spirit realm. Then we waited. Two days later, the large sum of money was suddenly wired to our account, as they had held an emergency meeting and for some reason had a change of heart.

GETTING RESULTS

Many people go to God but don't always get results. It is how we go to God that matters. If you need healing, you must go to God as the Healer. If you need deliverance, you go to Him as Deliverer. If you need the Father's love, you go to Him as a Father. What most Christians do when they are wronged and hurt is that they go to their Father with the problem and to get healed and loved out of the wounds. That works fine for the love portion, but when it comes to justice they need to go to God as Judge.

Imagine if your dad is a judge by profession. Let's say you come home at night to complain to him that someone cheated you and stole your house or car, and you have proof of who it is. Your dad would most likely comfort you, hold you, and give you advice. But legally, unless you go to court with your dad, there is not much he is authorized to do unless he is in his position and place as judge.

God will manifest in your life in the areas that you perceive Him. If you need healing, you don't go to God as Provider but as Healer. As you worship and know Him also as Judge, He can judge on your behalf. Most people think knowing Him as Judge is scary. But actually, if you come the right away, knowing Him in this way is a great thing.

Judgment day means you get what is coming to you. If you go to court and the judgment is that you were wronged and the enemy has to pay you back with recompense, then judgment day is a good day for you! That's why it's so key to first confess any known sins and repent of them, asking God to cleanse and forgive you. Once that is done, the devil has no legal right to use that sin against you in the courts of Heaven because it has already been paid for and confessed by the blood. He has nothing on you at this point. Jesus had that advantage: *"The prince of this world is coming. He has no hold over Me"* (John 14:30 NIV).

CITIES AND NATIONS

It is even possible to take an entire city or nation to the courts of Heaven. Recently, my wife and I were detained in a Russian airport upon arrival for one and a half hours. They took our passports and told us to wait as they looked through one of our suitcases filled with Christian books in both Russian and English we were bringing to believers there. They told us we would not be able to bring them in and said it was looking very bad. The situation got more and more tense as higher-level undercover security-type men and women came to inspect and start to read the materials, shaking their heads. They also began searching about us on their computers.

My wife reminded me that we should take our case quickly to the courts of Heaven to insure that we would even get to enter Russia. As we did, within five minutes of presenting our case, a lady ran to us and said, "You can go now. Go quickly!" She handed our passports back to us. I asked her why we were detained for so long and she only told us to just go—*now*! I don't know if there was a spiritual or prophetic correlation, but the famous NSA leaker, Edward Snowden, was released the same hour. We watched it on the news upon arriving at our hotel.

Even the prophet Daniel saw a major court case in process with the final verdict being the enemy of his cohorts being found guilty and sentenced. *"A river of fire was flowing, coming out from before Him. Thousands upon thousands attended Him; ten thousand times ten thousand stood before Him.* **The court was seated, and the books were opened***"* (Dan. 7:10 NIV).

In Daniel 9 we read about the time when Daniel counted the days when Israel should be set free from their oppressors. He began to fast and pray until he had a breakthrough. The archangel Gabriel was sent to give Daniel "insight and understanding." I believe he began to plead for Israel to be set free from her oppressors using the prophetic word that he had researched, which said that after the appointed years were up, Israel would be delivered. He pleaded his case, persisting until he got the breakthrough for Israel! Persistence for bigger cases is important, though many cases get immediate results.

I was in Hawaii speaking and the Lord showed me that a tsunami was coming to Hawaii and would have destroyed much of the islands with great loss of life. I began to pray and take it to the Judge of Heaven. I also sent a mass email to our intercessors to pray and fast. I had the native Hawaiian pastor and the church repent on behalf of Hawaii for certain statewide sins. We also repented for the passing of a new law that had just occurred, which was a law allowing gay couples to legally marry in Hawaii that week. We prayed, applied the blood, and asked God to diminish or cancel the tsunami. We saw souls saved, people bound by drugs delivered, healings, and miracles.

I boarded my plane to go home. As I arrived in California on my way to Arizona, I saw the news that while I was in the air Japan had the huge Tsunami preceded by earthquakes. Those same waves made their way to Maui where our meetings occurred, and to the other islands too. The entire street I was staying at had damage and was closed, as the waves overflowed the banks, causing millions of dollars of damage. But there was no loss of life. The experts were amazed that the destruction was not more widespread. Again, we were able to see destruction averted by taking it to the Judge of Heaven and earth.

Moses pleaded and reasoned with God, the Judge of Heaven and earth, why it would not be favorable to destroy the Jewish people in the desert (see Exod. 32:9-14). Had Moses not pleaded and argued his case, the nation of Israel and the Jewish people would not exist today.

Abraham attempted to negotiate his case for Sodom and Gomorrah, asking that God would spare it if there were ten righteous in the city (see Gen. 18:16-32). He stopped short of asking for five or three righteous people; if he had, he might have been able to win his case. Because the accuser knew there were not ten righteous people living there, Abraham lost that particular case.

We can argue our cases in a biblical way before the Judge of Heaven and see disaster averted, or at least greatly diminished. We can change events or the results of events by interceding our case before the Judge in the courts of Heaven. Yes, we know lots of these things are prophesied to occur in the last days, but we can intercede before the courts and see many lives saved, both physically and spiritually.

God desires that we come before Him so that He has a legal reason to avert and save instead of allowing those to perish by default because no one would come before Him to plead their case. The great thing about all this is that Jesus is our Advocate or lawyer (see 1 John 4:1). So we have an awesome Jewish Lawyer on our side! And guess what? The Judge is His Dad! Sounds like a pretty good deal to me.

Chapter 8

ANCIENT RESURRECTIONS

As it was in the days of Elijah, Elisha, and Jesus, so today a new release of resurrections will be seen as never before. Jesus commanded His disciples to raise the dead, heal the sick, and cleanse the leper—all in the same command. He didn't say only heal the sick, but when it comes to raising the dead, you really better think twice. No. Raising the dead is mentioned in the same way as healing the sick and casting out demons. Today's church has relegated resurrection ministry to the "not relevant" category, believing that it only happened in the days of the early church, or that it might happen once in a lifetime, or perhaps occasionally in far off, poor, developing countries.

In Ephesians, Paul prays that *"the God of our Lord Jesus Christ, the Father of glory, may give to you the spirit of wisdom and revelation in the knowledge of Him…that you may know… what is the exceeding greatness of His power toward us who believe, according to the working of His mighty power"* (Eph. 1:17-19).

The Lord will not only release His power to us, which He already has, but He will release revelation in order to know the workings of His power. It's no use having power without the knowledge about how to use it. I believe that God is revealing revelation knowledge in these days so believers will know not just the power, but how the power works—even for raising the dead.

God is restoring everything in these days, and will do so with even greater power. The spirit of Elijah will once again be fully resurrected in our day: *"Behold, I will send you Elijah the prophet before the coming of the great and dreadful day of the Lord"* (Mal. 4:5).

We know that some of the first major resurrections recorded involved Elijah and Elisha (see 1 Kings 17:17-24; 2 Kings 4:32-37). The pattern continued with Jesus, and, eventually, in the church. It is interesting to study the resurrections recorded in the Bible. In two similar circumstances, both Elijah and Elisha raised the dead in similar fashion. It would behoove us to learn from those who have already raised the dead.

> *And he stretched himself out on the child three times, and cried out to the Lord and said, "O Lord my God, I pray, let this child's soul come back to him." Then the Lord heard the voice of Elijah; and the soul of the child came back to him, and he revived* (1 Kings 17:21-22).

This major miracle in Elijah's ministry launched him into a new realm. When Elisha was confronted with the same situation later in his ministry, he naturally raised the dead in the same way he knew his spiritual father had. As Elisha was a student of Elijah, it would be normal that Elijah at some point would have told the story of how he raised the dead. This also would have been the talk of the nation for years, as it had never occurred before. So Elisha should have been very knowledgeable about how Elijah, his spiritual father and tutor, raised the dead.

Look carefully at the next passage, which gives us more detail than the account in First Kings, and observe how Elisha raised the dead:

> *And he went up and lay on the child, and put his mouth on his mouth, his eyes on his eyes, and his hands on his hands; and he stretched himself out on the child, and the flesh of the child became warm. He returned and walked back and forth in the house, and again went up and stretched himself out on him; then the child sneezed seven times, and the child opened his eyes* (2 Kings 4:34-35).

There are several keys to raising the dead, as we can see in the Elijah and Elisha accounts. Both of them stretched out their bodies on the dead boys. The Scripture explains that Elisha put his mouth on the boy's mouth, as well as his eyes and hands on the boy's eyes and hands. Why in the world would someone put their mouth on a dead person's mouth? This ancient pathway to resurrections exists in part today in the secular world in the procedure known as mouth-to-mouth resuscitation, which sometimes works to revive a person who has stopped breathing. But where did this idea originate?

Life was breathed into the Adam's nostrils by God (see Gen. 2:7). God symbolically put His face to Adam's face and brought life to him. This Genesis account may have been a source of direction, revelation, and inspiration for Elijah.

What God did was breathe "spirit" into man. A person with only a body but no human spirit has no life. Life is in the spirit of a person. When someone dies, the spirit of the person departs from the body. If the human spirit returns to the body, life returns. We see this principle in Ezekiel:

> *Also He said to me, "Prophesy to the breath, prophesy, son of man, and say to the breath, 'Thus says the Lord God: "Come from the four winds, O breath, and breathe on these slain, that they may live.""" So I prophesied as He commanded me, and breath came into them, and they lived, and stood upon their feet, an exceedingly great army* (Ezekiel 37:9-10).

The word *breath* in God's command to the prophet is really translated as "spirit" when translated literally from the original Hebrew. The spirit of a man or woman returning to their body is the key to raising the dead. That is why Elijah prayed, *"Oh, Lord, let this child's soul come back to him."* He was calling the child's spirit back into his body.

The differences between translations became clear to me when I was preaching in Quebec, Canada, which I explained in greater detail earlier in this book in the chapter on supernatural wisdom. An English Bible I was reading before said He commanded breath, but the French Bible said He commanded their spirit to return to them, not just breath. As I was preaching, I received a revelation. I preached this revelation as it was coming to me while in the pulpit. All of a sudden a glory for raising the dead was released into the room—I could sense it so strongly.

One revelation from God is all it takes to see a new manifestation of His abundant glory. Don't ever forget that a new revelation brings a new manifestation of God. We need to continually seek God for fresher and clearer revelation and for a greater and more powerful manifestation of God's glory in the world in these last days.

NO DISTANCE IN THE SPIRIT

Another time I was holding an outdoor crusade in Africa. During the service I received a word from the Lord that a lady in the crowd had come to the meeting by faith, yet her daughter was dying in a nearby hospital. Then I received a word from the Lord that the girl had just died but that we were to pray her back to life from where we were. When I spoke that word out, the mother began to weep. From the pulpit, I commanded the spirit of the girl to come back into her body even though she was not physically at the meeting.

After the service, the mother ran to the hospital to see what had become of her daughter. The doctor said while the mother was gone she died and was no longer breathing, and then explained that they realized later she had come back to life. Time wise, she started breathing shortly after we began commanding her spirit to come back into her body. In this case I did not personally need to be in the same room to see the dead raised, as there is no distance in the glory. Since there is no distance in the spirit, we can command things to happen far away from us. Jesus commanded the Roman centurion's servant to be healed without setting foot in his house—and the same hour his servant was healed (see Luke 7:1-10).

Not Dead, Only Sleeping

Our friend Lazarus sleeps, but I go that I may wake him up (John 11:11).

How could Jesus tell them that Lazarus was not dead when clearly by all human measures he was as dead as any other corpse? What was the revelation behind all this, and how did He raise him from the dead? Earlier in the passage, Jesus said that the sickness was not unto death but for the glory of God (see John 11:4). Lazarus was Jesus's friend. He, along with Lazarus's sisters, Mary and Martha, spent much time together. Lazarus was well acquainted with the power and life of Jesus.

One day while I was preaching in one of our miracle campaigns, this revelation hit me right before I went up to the microphone—Jesus was able to speak to Lazarus even though he was physically dead. How was Jesus able to speak to him? Because Lazarus knew Jesus. After the life of Jesus touches a life and breathes on it, it can never die. Because you have a living, personal relationship with the Messiah, you will never die. Lazarus was not dead—he knew Jesus. All Jesus needed to do was wake him up from his sleep. The proof that he was not dead, at least in the spiritual sense, is that Lazarus responded by obeying Jesus and came back into his body.

Anything that God has breathed upon receives life; it may seem dead, but it is only in a sleeping state. Because Lazarus's life was totally devoted to God's Kingdom, Jesus could easily pull him from Heaven to earth. When God has touched something in your life, it never dies, even if it seems like it is not moving. Has God spoken or prophesied some things over your life that once had life but now seem dead? Did God use you powerfully in a certain way, and now it seems to be lost or gone? Those gifts and prophecies are not dead. If God ever breathed upon an area of your life, it is not dead; it is only sleeping. Wake it up! Did God heal you, and you seem to have lost that healing? It is not lost, only sleeping, because He has already touched it. Maybe you have unfulfilled promises. If they were "God-breathed," then they are not dead.

Even Abraham had faith that God would raise Isaac from the dead if he had to go through with killing him as a sacrifice (see Gen. 22:1-18). Why? Because he knew that God had already breathed life and destiny on the boy; he knew that God cannot lie and that God is life, even in the face of death.

Even the promise to give Abraham a son at his ridiculous age had to come to life. His body and the body of his wife were as good as dead, yet God spoke life to their bodies and a son, Isaac, was born (see Gen. 21:1-3). There is nothing that God has ever touched that now appears dead that He can't awaken. Believers in the Kingdom of God never really die, as we are made alive in Christ whether in the body or spirit.

I believe that as you read this, God will reveal some promises that you thought He had forgotten about or allowed to die. But in reality He is just waiting for you to realize that your dream, prophecy, revelation, desire, or miracle is not dead—it is only sleeping. He is ready to awaken those promises as you open yourself to His abundant glory.

Even cities and countries that once had major revivals and now seem dead are not dead, because the ashes of that revival still remain in the ground. In France, for example, tens of thousands died as martyrs for their faith during the civil wars, and even before. They were called the French Huguenots. France, a country many have identified as spiritually dead, has never been dead, only sleeping; and is now awakening with major miracles being witnessed, souls being saved, and churches growing.

There is a suburb of Paris called St. Denis where the World Cup Soccer tournament was played. In the subway station, there is a statue of a man holding his head in his hand; his name is St. Denis. He was a believer who preached with such conviction that the religious leaders of his day had him beheaded. It is written that St. Denis picked up his head and walked several miles from the place of execution back to the very church that ordered his death. I believe he was not really dead because God had touched him.[34]

God has manifested His resurrection glory in times past in different ways, and today is no different because God never changes.

THE SAME YESTERDAY, TODAY, AND TOMORROW

Across the United States, Europe, and many other western nations, the abundant glory and power of God is once again resurrecting and waking up what was and continues to be.

Several years ago I ministered in Spokane, Washington, where John G. Lake ministered healing to the whole city. People came to his healing rooms where they would be prayed for and where they remained until they were healed. The basic idea was that everyone who entered stayed as long as it took until healing took place. To prove the point, Spokane was rated the healthiest city in America by secular standards.[35]

I visited Mr. Lake's gravesite and noticed a pine tree growing right through his grave. While preaching, I saw a vision of

John G. Lake being raised from the dead. The Lord showed me that his anointing and ministry did not die when he passed away and that it would be resurrected if someone would just pick up the mantle that is lying on the ground in Spokane.

The glory that touched the city and seemed to have faded away was actually sleeping, waiting for someone else to wake it up. A short time later, I learned that Cal Pierce had bought the property and renamed it the "healing rooms," and the healing ministry of John G. Lake is continuing today right where it started. The mantle never died; it just waited for someone with the revelation to awaken it.

After God has breathed on an area, a city, a ministry, or anything, it only sleeps; it never truly dies. Wake it up! Stir up the gifts that are in you, and stir up the mantles over your region. God is unleashing the Elijah glory with resurrection power to raise bodies, ministries, families, and nations from the dead!

RESURRECTION GLORY AND ISRAEL

The early church walked in a level of resurrection glory and power that we have yet to see. What was their secret? How did they tap into this extreme glory? The Bible talks about the spirit of Elijah being restored in the last days:

> *Behold, I will send you Elijah the prophet before the coming of the great and dreadful day of the Lord. And he will turn the hearts of the fathers to the children, and the hearts of the children to their fathers, lest I come and strike the earth with a curse* (Malachi 4:5-6).

Here we see the return of the spirit of Elijah connected to the hearts of fathers turning to their children and the children to their fathers. The Jewish people are the spiritual fathers of the faith. The Gentile church today is the children and offspring of the Jewish apostles and prophets. We have been disconnected from each other for over 2,000 years. As we are reconnected to each other, the resurrection power of God that the early church walked in will be unlocked.

The church was cut off from her Jewish roots in A.D. 325 during the Council of Nicaea, and ever since that time the power and visitation of God has been diminished compared to what it was in the early church. I believe it was actually lifted from the church for a long season. As we reconnect to the Jewish roots of the gospel, we will draw from the rich soil of God's power. Paul clearly demonstrates this in his writings in the Book of Romans: *"For if their being cast away is the reconciling of the world, what will their acceptance be but life from the dead?"* (Rom. 11:15).

Here we see Paul talking about the raising of the dead in connection with Israel as the Jewish people are restored to salvation in their God. When Israel, the root, is restored to the Messiah, and we are connected to that root of Israel and our Jewish forefathers, it will be as the raising of the dead for us and our ministries. God is about to unleash a wave of resurrection glory to those ministries and churches that will reconnect to the root and help Israel return to her Messiah. They will be accepted as they come; they will also function as a hedge of protection. The early church started with all Jewish believers and later opened to Gentiles. That dynamic allowed for an explosion of God's power as the two became one in Him.

A flower cut from its roots can only survive two days before it starts to die. The church today has been uprooted and on its own for 2,000 years without connection to Israel. We think we can continue the way we have been, but the third day is coming, and we cannot survive unless we get reconnected to our Jewish roots. A day is as a thousand years to the Lord—we are now entering the third day (see 2 Pet. 3:8).

On the third day Jesus rose from the dead. If the early Gentile church under Constantine cut themselves off from Israel and their Jewish brethren and began the spiral of loss of supernatural power and effectiveness over the church, then it would seem normal for believers and ministries who are not reconnecting to Israel and its revival and influencing their followers to pray for, bless, and prepare Israel for the coming harvest, to also avoid the stagnation of the anointing, blessing, and favor. Paul foresaw this danger as he wrote to the Gentile church headquartered in Rome at the time, saying,

> For I do not desire, brethren, that you should be
> ignorant of this mystery, lest you should be wise
> in your own opinion, that blindness in part has
> happened to Israel until the fullness of the Gentiles
> has come in. And so all Israel will be saved, as it is
> written... (Romans 11:25-26).

Paul also admonished, *"Do not boast against the branches. But if you do boast, remember that you do not support the root, but the root supports you"* (Rom. 11:18). As more and more in the Gentile church across different streams and denominational lines are starting to pray for and bless Israel, the forefathers of the faith, God is starting to also bring life, revival, and refreshing to the entire tree of the body of believers worldwide.

I believe those who support the revival of Israel will be part of a third-day wave of great resurrection glory, power, favor, prosperity, and harvest.

> *I say then, have they stumbled that they should fall? Certainly not! But through their fall, to provoke them to jealousy, salvation has come to the Gentiles. Now if their fall is riches for the world, and their failure riches for the Gentiles, how much more their fullness!* (Romans 11:11-12)

What a great reason to pray and be a part of the revival of Israel, so that the fullness of what God has for the nations and our ministries comes to pass. Paul clearly explains in Romans that God's plan is to show Israel mercy once again, just as He has shown mercy to the church that has also been disobedient. God wants to create "one new man," Jew and Gentile as one in Him (see Eph. 2:15). When that happens, it will unleash a worldwide wave of glory that we have yet to see. Let it begin today in your life and ministry.

ISRAEL'S RESURRECTION

In the Book of Ezekiel, there is mention of a valley of dry bones coming back together, and then being raised from the dead. Many use this passage to preach to the church about arising out of slumber and lukewarmness, but I believe this passage is actually referring to Israel today. It can be applied to the church after it has been properly applied first to Israel to whom it was originally written.

> *So I prophesied as He commanded me, and breath came into them, and they lived, and stood upon*

their feet, an exceedingly great army. Then He said
to me, "Son of man, these bones are the whole house
of Israel. They indeed say, 'Our bones are dry, our
hope is lost, and we ourselves are cut off!'" (Ezekiel
37:10-11)

This is clearly a picture of the Jewish people, the whole
house of Israel, who had no homeland and had been scattered and lost. But God is beginning to resurrect and gather
His chosen.

In 1948 the nation of Israel was established and is now
in the middle of world events. It is evident that Israel, God's
chosen people, is a vital link to the future of the nations. The
Hebrew language has also been resurrected after 2,000 years,
as Israel was destroyed by the Romans, and the Jews only got
back control of Israel in 1948 and once again made Hebrew the
official language. Most Jews did not know Hebrew because it
was not spoken for so many years as the Jews lived in foreign
lands, speaking different languages until the rebirth of modern-
day Israel.

How does all this relate to moving in resurrection power?
The resurrection of Israel and her revival will unleash the last
great worldwide harvest of souls and bring resurrection glory
back to believers. As we accept and participate in what God
is doing for His chosen people, the entire body of believers in
Jesus will reap the same resurrection glory that is occurring
with Israel as a nation.

Therefore prophesy and say to them, "Thus says
the Lord God: 'Behold, O My people, I will open
your graves and cause you to come up from your

*graves, and bring you into the land of Israel. Then
you shall know that I am the Lord, when I have
opened your graves, O My people, and brought you
up from your graves. I will put My Spirit in you,
and you shall live, and I will place you in your own
land. Then you shall know that I, the Lord, have
spoken it and performed it,' says the Lord"* (Ezekiel
37:12-14).

Wow, what an exciting time we live in. Ezekiel says that
God is opening their graves and bringing them back to their
land, Israel. This is already beginning to happen; many Jews
are moving to Israel, but there are many more who want and
need to go home to Israel. Ezekiel commanded the bones to
come together, and flesh came on them, but there was no
spirit or breath in them. I believe that as soon as the remnants
of God's chosen people return to Israel, their homeland, God
will start to breathe His Spirit upon them and bring national
revival. This will, in turn, cause global revival.

Many from the United States and western Europe, where
the majority of Jews reside today, are moving back to Israel.
France is the second largest population of Jews living outside
of Israel, with over 600,000. They are next to the U.S., which
has the most Jews worldwide according to world Jewish population statistics. More Jews returned to Israel from France in
2005 alone than they had in 35 years. That year 3,300 French
Jews immigrated to Israel, making a move called *Aliyah*, which
refers to Jews returning to their biblical homeland. Between
2001 and 2005, over 11,148 Jews make *Aliyah* to Israel from
France. This was partly due to the second Intifada in Israel
and anti-Semitic acts that have greatly risen in France. The

Human Rights Commission reported that in 2002 there were six times more anti-Semitic acts against French Jews than the previous year, and these constituted 62 percent of all racist acts in the country.

There are also approximately 110,000 North American immigrants in Israel, and the flow has been steady since 1948. Record numbers arrived in the late 1960s and '70s after the Six-Day War. Another record of North American Jews moving to Israel occurred also in 2005 after the Intifada, the highest number since 1983, though the reasons are not because of persecution or finances but more for solidarity, ideological, political, or spiritual reasons.[36]

Recently, Jewish agency officials announced that the Jewish state may be on the threshold of a new wave of North American immigrants. They suggested this is due to Israel's strong economy compared to dipping stock markets and the growing financial crunch in the U.S. An immigrant spokeswoman said there is fear of a growing recession in the U.S. compared to an optimistic outlook for Israel's future, especially in high-tech industries. Around 3,000 new immigrants are expected from North America by the end of 2008.[37]

If one day, God forbid, people in America ever turned against the Jewish people, and persecution arose because of world events on television regarding Israel or a downward economy blamed on Israel or the Jews, I believe God will prepare believers like you and me to help them on their journey to return to Israel, just like Corrie ten Boom helped many Jews escape persecution during World War II. But how will Christians be prepared unless they have a revelation of their calling to be a blessing to the Jewish people in the last days?

As you are praying them home, also help them with their move to Israel, support ministries that help them, reach out to them in Israel and at home, and stand up for them in their time of persecution. Then you too will partake of the greatest wave of power, revival, and glory that has ever been experienced.

BLESSING ISRAEL

When we began to bless Israel, our lives and entire ministry changed dramatically. First, we toured Israel—which I recommend every believer do at least once in their lifetime. While on our first trip to Israel in 1994, we were visited in the Upper Room by the Holy Spirit. Also during the trip, my wife and I led 13 Israelis to the Messiah. Having blessed Israel with souls saved and with the outpouring we received in the Upper Room, God rewarded us with nonstop revival for the next five years leading up to a six-month nightly revival with souls saved daily, miracles, and signs.

In 1999, the Lord told us to go again to Israel and pour out the glory of God that we were experiencing afresh with demonstrations of power to the congregations and churches there. We were able to impart what God had given us, and the ministries we ministered to began to move in great power, signs, and wonders. Due to this, God told us He would enlarge our ministry because we had deposited His glory into a larger arena in Israel. During the next two years, we held large glory/miracle campaigns across Europe, Africa, the United States, and other nations, with many extraordinary miracles resulting and many more salvations. God also opened television opportunities for us, and we were able to purchase our own property and ministry base in Europe to reach the nations on that side of the world, in addition to our U.S. ministry.

In February 2003, we took a team of 50 people to Israel. As we toured and held meetings, Israelis streamed through the doors asking if they could join our singing—they said they felt so happy when they were with us. We rejoiced with them as they rediscovered their Jewish Messiah. During this trip we met with Israeli government officials; we blessed them, prayed for them, repented for the western church's history of anti-Semitism, and resolved to stand with Israel with a declaration signed by many believers abroad. The government officials were moved to tears and vowed to give this resolution of support for Israel to the prime minister at the time, Ariel Sharon. This was one of our first steps in reconnecting with Israel, returning to our roots, and standing with the nation of Israel in her time of need.

I believe that in this next, and maybe final, move of God, any ministry or believer who does not have some type of emphasis on blessing, praying for, sharing the Messiah with, or loving Israel and the Jewish people in these last days will miss out on the most exciting events in history, the revival, and the harvest, and they could also begin to notice a dwindling of influence and favor. The Bible clearly explains that when the full number of the Gentiles comes in, then all Israel will be saved. At the moment, most Gentile nations are experiencing a greater level of salvation worldwide and more and more Jews in Israel are receiving the Messiah as we have witnessed firsthand on many occasions and through the many reports of believers living there. So why would we want to miss out on the most exciting harvest fields of both the Gentiles and the final harvest of Jews coming to salvation?

Paul, the Jewish apostle to the Gentiles, warned the Gentile believers blessed by the gospel ever so clearly, *"I speak to you Gentiles; inasmuch as I am an apostle to the Gentiles, I magnify my ministry"* (Rom 11:13). He continues on and says what many believers began to conclude and many still do: that because the Jewish religious leaders denied the gospel, God basically gave all the blessings and rights to the Gentile believers. This almost gave them a sense of superiority and lack of compassion or burden for their Jewish brethren that gave them the gospel in the first place. Paul tells the Gentile church, *"You will say then, 'Branches were broken off that I might be grafted in.' Well said. Because of unbelief they were broken off, and you stand by faith. Do not be haughty, but fear. For if God did not spare the natural branches He might not spare you either"* (Rom. 11:19-22).

Paul warned of pride and haughtiness toward Israel and the Jews. It is true that one cannot have a burden or calling for every nation, but I believe that the Scriptures are pretty clear that there is one nation in particular that every believer is asked to pray for and help, and that is Israel. There are many other reasons to pray for and bless them. To just name a few, Israel was the first to bring the gospel of Jesus to the Gentiles, and we owe them that debt of gratitude. Romans clearly points out that the Gentiles are to make Israel and the Jews jealous again for their Messiah, not to mention that the Word of God commands believers to pray for Israel. The debt we owe the Jewish people is enormous, as without them the church would have no patriarchs, no apostles, no Bible, and no Savior. There are other books dedicated to this very subject of the pros and cons of blessing and not blessing Israel, our spiritual parents.

Honor your father and your mother, as the Lord your God has commanded you, that your days may be long, and that it may be well with you in the land which the Lord your God is giving you (Deuteronomy 5:16).

As we honor Israel and the Jewish people by praying for their salvation, awakening, and revival, and blessing them in their time of need, God promises to also unleash the spirit of Elijah, where resurrection power occurred and was demonstrated again through Jesus. People often speak about honoring our fathers and mothers of the faith of days gone by and honoring spiritual parents like our pastors and those who mentored us. As the Word tells us to honor our parents, we need to apply this to our spiritual parents—Israel and the Jewish people.

As we enter the third day, God wants us to return to our early church roots and the first few hundred years of its greatest glory. This reconnection is a major aspect of the "Elijah glory" in these last days, restoring the foundation on which we stand as He restores the spirit of Elijah, turning the hearts of the children to the fathers and the fathers to the children.

Pray for the peace of Jerusalem: "May they prosper who love you. Peace be within your walls, prosperity within your palaces." For the sake of my brethren and companions, I will now say, "Peace be within you." Because of the house of the Lord our God, I will seek your good (Psalm 122:6-9).

Chapter 9

ELISHA'S DOUBLE PORTION

This chapter is taken from my book *Glory Invasion* because of the relevant content within this context.

And so it was, when they had crossed over,
that Elijah said to Elisha, "Ask! What may I do
for you, before I am taken away from you?"
Elisha said, "Please let a double portion
of your spirit be upon me" (2 KINGS 2:9).

Elisha wanted to be just like his spiritual father, Elijah. That is the reason he asked for a double portion of his anointing when he left. Elisha wanted to continue the legacy so Elijah, in a sense, would live on through the same glory, yet stronger. It is recorded that Elijah performed seven major miracles—Elisha is credited with fourteen. The last one was after his death. His bones so held the glory and sound waves of power that, when a dead man was thrown onto Elisha's bones in the same grave, the man was instantly resurrected (see 2 Kings 13:21).

The *"Elisha glory"* is when the torch of the last generation is passed to the next generation with even greater power. To operate in this realm, there are some important principles to understand. Recently, several spiritual leaders and apostles of the faith have gone on to be with the Lord—now is the time to walk into the Elisha mantle and continue where they left off.

To do this we must be willing to stand with those we consider our spiritual leaders when they are attacked or criticized. This is the true test of our love and friendship. When we are a close friend to those leaders who are being promoted, blessed, and honored, it is easy to want to be part of their company. But the test comes during persecution.

The disciples were severely tested. Judas wanted what he could get from Jesus's popularity. He wanted the same power for miracles, esteem in the eyes of others, and a place in the government next to Jesus when He would, supposedly, overthrow the Roman government. Of course Judas did not realize that it was the spiritual Kingdom of God on the earth that Jesus was implementing at that time. When Judas and the others realized that the fun part was over and that Jesus was going to be mocked, scourged, crucified, and humiliated, they had second thoughts about openly demonstrating their association with Jesus. When you know someone and his or her true heart, it does not matter what a critic says, or what is written claiming otherwise. This will be the place of promotion or demotion, depending on our stand in that moment.

This is going to be the model for the true apostolic wave that is coming: believers who are willing to lay down their lives for those God has appointed them to serve—and, ultimately, for the Lord Jesus Himself. The disciples left all to follow Jesus, and Jesus said to them *that they "will do even greater things than these, because I go to the Father"* (John 14:12 AMP).

That is when the double portion comes, when we receive the spiritual inheritance of our fathers in the faith because we were faithful to serve and honor them. Elisha left all to follow Elijah, a type of Jesus, and he received the "greater things"—a double-portion anointing—and gave God all the glory.

Few people in our day have really tapped into the double portion of what the church saw even 50 years ago with regard to the glory, power, and miracles. Why is this? Few today have even the *same* portion as Kathryn Kuhlman, A. A. Allen, or Jack Coe—just to name a few of the great healing evangelists of the 1950s.

RUTH HEFLIN

I was blessed to know Ruth Heflin, a prophet and apostolic leader and minister. She was like Elijah in the sense that she was a prophetess unto the Lord like none other I have ever seen. She prophesied and spoke the word of the Lord to many presidents around the world. She moved in signs and wonders and often glistened with "glory dust." With one prophecy alone, she would totally turn your world upside down, and the prophecy would begin happening as she was speaking it. Just by being around her, I felt like my entire walk with God was thrown into a supernatural acceleration, taking me years ahead of my time.

She treated my wife and me like family and friends from the first day we met. We ministered with her in her special camp meetings and also received great impartations through her ministry, yet there was another element that was totally different from the impartations we received over the years. It was the immense love she had for us and those around her. I knew she loved me as a son, and that made all the difference in the world. When she came under attack and was criticized for the new things or revelation she was having—as she was usually ahead of her time, but in God's perfect time—we always felt compelled to stand with her and continue to show that she was our mother in the Lord and role model, even if it meant we would receive some of the persecution. Sometimes she was very popular, and at other times she took a different stand from all the others.

I remember seeing her pray with tears for President Bill Clinton and telling me that he would not be impeached and would be reelected because God had a plan. It had nothing to do with whether or not he deserved it. God simply told Ruth that it would have adverse effects on the United States, our economy, and the gospel going out from the U.S. if he were taken out of office in such a way at that particular time.

One thing was sure, because she prayed for him and many other government officials, she was often invited by the president to come and share the word of the Lord with him. Many other presidents and dignitaries invited her as well. Doors were open to her because she prayed for people, not against them. She would not allow her tongue to destroy a person of authority, but instead prayed for those in authority despite their beliefs or sin.

We decided to do likewise and pray for President Clinton to change. We prayed that he would repent publicly on national television. Sometimes you must not go with the crowd if you want to keep that anointing, even when your own reasoning does not understand what is happening. Soon after our prayers, he was on television repenting.

Ruth was used to birth a new revival of the glory of God and signs and wonders. In her camp meetings, every imaginable sign and wonder took place, which, of course, ruffled the feathers of those comfortable with the status quo. We again staked our ground and said that we were part of this new wave of God. We saw many souls saved and multitudes healed; governments began to open up to us around the world, and the blessings continue to this day.

Ruth became very ill after a car accident, and soon enough she went to be with the Lord. We had just been with her weeks before. In fact, the weekend she died she was scheduled to minister with me in a big conference in The Hague in Holland. I arrived at the conference without Ruth, and the pastor asked me where she was. When I told him she had passed away, he told me I would have to speak during her sessions as well as mine. I did not know what to say.

How could I fill her shoes when others were expecting her to speak? The Lord showed me about walking in her shoes and mantle in a greater way. I was to minister in her sessions under her anointing as well as mine. I was to walk into the "double portion," which included the anointing and glory that I was faithful to steward upon my own life as well as the inheritance of some of her anointing, grace, and glory. As I ministered the glory, the prophetic, signs and wonders, and salvations, the glory doubled and multiplied like I had never seen before—and that was only the beginning.

During the conference, which ended on a Sunday, the Lord told me to go to Ruth's funeral. The only problem: the funeral was in the U.S. on Tuesday, and I was returning to France on Monday from Holland to rejoin my wife and kids who were awaiting my return. I told the Lord how hard it would be to leave Holland by Monday, take a train to France, and then find a plane ticket at the last minute on the same day. I explained to the Lord that I had just been with Ruth a few weeks before. The Lord told me that I had to see her off until the end, as Elisha stayed with Elijah until the end, to receive the double portion. The Lord impressed upon me that it was of utter importance that I go, no matter the cost.

I quickly called the airlines and miraculously found a ticket. I rushed to France, grabbed my wife, and rushed to the airport where we almost missed our flight. That night upon arriving in the U.S., I was in Ashland, Virginia, where her body lay the night before the funeral. As we walked in the room, the glory was so thick that we began to weep—not just because she had passed away, but because of the intense glory that filled the room. It was stronger than when she was alive. I asked the Lord how this could be. Then He explained to me the passage in which even the bones of Elisha had raised a man from the dead. The glory was so strong on his own physical body that a dead man could be raised by touching it (see 2 Kings 13:21).

The Lord told me to touch her body, and a double portion would be imparted. As she was now in a higher realm of glory in Heaven, her body was the point of contact to transmit the glory between Heaven and earth. As we laid our hands upon her body, the power of God shot though us like an electrical surge that can only be explained as resurrection glory. Little did we know that we would be sitting next to our new glory friends, Mahesh and Bonnie Chavda. They also received a mighty impartation and inheritance from Ruth. This was another reason God sent us, so He could direct us to our next covenant relationship in His glory. Since then we have seen a much greater glory and definitely at least a double portion of what we had before this trip.

THE MASTER KEY TO THE DOUBLE PORTION

I have noticed something important about those who walk with the greatest mantles—they also honor Israel and the Jewish people who are the spiritual parents of all believers and the church.

As mentioned previously, as we honor our spiritual parents—Israel and the Jewish people—God promises a special blessing. In fact, in these last days, those who honor Israel and the Jewish people have in the past and can today receive a double-portion blessing. In Malachi, the spirit of Elijah being restored is connected to the hearts of the fathers (Israel) turning to their children, and the hearts of the children (the church) turning to their fathers (see Mal. 4:6). How can we receive a double portion of what the early church had if we don't identify, honor, and associate ourselves with them and their offspring today? It will require us to stand firm with Israel in her time of crises when it is not popular to do so.

Ministries that are sincerely praying, fasting, and interceding for our spiritual parents—Israel and the Jews who birthed us into the faith—will experience a whole new dimension in God. God is also calling many to support the work of God in Israel and simply identify with them.

> *Many of the people of Israel are now enemies of the Good News, and this benefits you Gentiles. Yet they are still the people He loves because He chose their ancestors Abraham, Isaac, and Jacob. For God's gifts and His call can never be withdrawn* (Romans 11:28-29 NLT).

We see a generational blessing that doubles and multiplies. Abraham, blessed by God, left a spiritual inheritance to his son Isaac. Isaac was born with an already-blessed status from his father; in addition, whatever else he would do for God would add to that blessing. Each generation that honored its fathers received an even greater blessing. Jacob received the blessings of Abraham and that of his own father Isaac, plus whatever else he would be and do for God.

If we cut ourselves off from identifying with the Jewish people, we lose that generational blessing and are cut off from the root of where the blessings began. The blessings came out of Abraham and the Jewish people. As we recognize how we have been grafted in, and become *"a partaker of the root and fatness of the olive tree,"* we tap into all the blessings from the time of Abraham to Jesus, the early church, and even today (Rom. 11:17). Take a strong stand with your forefather Israel and see the inheritance and double portion come upon you. Incorporate intercession for Israel and the Jewish people around the world, for their salvation, protection, and their return to the land of their forefathers.

JUDEO-CHRISTIAN HERITAGE

Esther is a type of the church. She had a good position in life and favor with the king. The church is often in this place, especially in the West. We are living off of the blessings that our forefathers laid down for us. Many of us are comfortable, and things are going fairly well. But there is a problem. The king knows not that Esther is a Jew, and now there is an extermination decree (see Esther 2:10; 3:12-15). She is in a desperate position. Will she go before the king and risk losing her position, esteem, prosperity, and even her life by identifying herself with the Jews? It was known in Esther's day that anyone who went before the king without permission would be executed. Furthermore, how would the king respond to her request to annul the declaration to kill the entire Jewish race?

She had two options. She could stay and do nothing and continue receiving the benefits of a queen, or she could do something about it. Mordecai told her that she was born, blessed, and honored in her present position for a purpose: *"Yet who knows whether you have come to the kingdom for such a time as this?"* (Esther 4:14).

In other words, the only reason God blessed and favored her in such a way was so she could use this favor to bless Israel. If she failed, she would have missed the reason for her existence, an Israelite blessed in order to be a blessing to Israel. She chose to reveal her true identity to the king. We too must reveal our true identity as children of God and offspring of Israel. Will we be silent in these days when it is unpopular to stand with Israel and the Jewish people, or will we reveal that we are one with Israel and honor our spiritual fathers of the faith and Jesus Himself who came as a Jew?

The United States and Europe are facing this same dilemma. The nations that have experienced great revival in Christendom are among the most blessed and respected nations in the world. Will America and her allies stand by Israel and the Jews, knowing that their blessings originated when they helped Israel become a nation again and became a refuge for many Jews? Or will we close our eyes and try to be politically correct so as to avoid future enemy attacks? If we don't take a strong stand with those who initiated our blessing, we will eventually lose what we are trying to save. We must once again stand with the root of our blessing and spiritual inheritance instead of cutting off our root system in hopes of self-preservation.

> *And if some of the branches were broken off, and you, being a wild olive tree, were grafted in among them, and with them became a partaker of the root and fatness of the olive tree, do not boast against the branches. But if you do boast, remember that you do not support the root, but the root supports you* (Romans 11:17-18).

Joseph had a similar testing to that facing today's western nations. Although a Jew, he became great in the Gentile nation of Egypt. He used his favored position not just for himself but to also save Israel from starvation (see Gen. 45:7). He revealed his true identity and his association with his brothers and Israel. Moses also did the same and chose rather to suffer affliction with God's people than to enjoy the pleasures of sin in the house of Pharaoh. Receiving the double portion of God's glory and anointing rests heavily upon this principle of revealing your identity with God's chosen people.

Ruth followed Naomi, her Jewish mother-in-law, and God blessed her for it. She identified herself with Naomi and told her, *"Wherever you go, I will go...your people shall be my people, and your God, my God"* (Ruth 1:16). That is what you call identifying with Israel. Ruth was a Gentile, yet followed and identified with her Jewish mother-in-law. She eventually met Boaz, a type of Christ, who was to be her husband. Boaz gave her a double portion of the grain that the others were receiving when he heard about her sacrifice and love for her mother-in-law. Ruth is even in the family lineage of Jesus. We too will reap a double portion Elisha anointing of everything that God has planned to give us if we honor our spiritual father, Israel, in these last days, and use our favor, finances, gifts, and anointing to bless Israel and prepare her to accept her Messiah.

Cornelius was a Gentile who supported Israel, and God blessed him spiritually as Peter came to his house and brought salvation and an outpouring of the Holy Spirit to the first Gentile convert (see Acts 10). The Bible also mentions the Roman centurion of whom they said, *"He loves our nation, and has built us a synagogue"* (Luke 7:5). Jesus was drawn to bless him when He learned how the Roman helped the Jewish people, and He granted his request:

> *And when the centurion heard of Jesus, he sent some Jewish elders to Him, requesting Him to come and make his bond servant well. And when they reached Jesus, they begged him earnestly, saying, He is worthy that You should do this for him, for he loves our nation and he built us our synagogue [at his own expense]. And Jesus went with them* (Luke 7:3-6 AMP).

THE DOUBLE PORTION
AND THE FIRSTBORN

Tradition demanded that the firstborn son receive a double portion of the inheritance and blessing of the father. That is why Esau and Jacob fought from their birth until the day Esau sold his birthright and regretted it later. I believe the Lord is about to release a firstborn double portion now to those who are attentive and seeking it.

The first to be born into the Kingdom were the Jews. From the Old Testament and in the New Testament, they were the first to receive the commandments, to be called His people, to receive salvation and the baptism of the Holy Spirit. As they are the firstborn, God promises some things to them. Isaiah 60-62 speaks of the restoration of Israel and the Jews to their land and to their God:

> *And they shall rebuild the old ruins, they shall raise up the former desolations, and they shall repair the ruined cities, the desolations of many generations. Strangers shall stand and feed your flocks, and the sons of the foreigner shall be your plowmen and your vinedressers* (Isaiah 61:4-5).

Here we see what is already coming to pass in our day as the Jewish people have begun to return and restore the nation that was practically in ruins. The next verse gets more exciting:

> *Instead of your shame you shall have double honor, and instead of confusion they shall rejoice in their*

portion. Therefore in their land they shall possess
double; everlasting joy shall be theirs (Isaiah 61:7).

God promises a double portion to the Jewish people above
all the other nations and people of the earth. If we identify
with them as Ruth did with Naomi, we too will receive a
double portion and fully enter into the Elisha anointing. If
we identify ourselves with Israel and make it known that we
are of the same family, whether it produces blessing or persecution, we are saying that we are joined with the firstborn. I
believe that if we look at Israel as if it is also our land—at least
spiritually—and if we intercede and fast and pray for the Jews
around the world to know the Messiah, we will also be considered by God as the firstborn.

Jacob disguised himself as his older brother, Esau, to receive
firstborn status and blessing from his blind father. Because
his father could not tell the difference as he smelled, felt, and
almost talked like his brother, he gave Jacob the blessing. We
must identify with the firstborn and God's purposes in the
earth for them so that we ourselves become mistaken for being
the firstborn and receive a double portion.

But if we make a distinction between "us and them," we
will miss the double portion blessing. If we say we are the
church and we are now the beloved apple of God's eye, apart
from Israel and the Jews, then we lose our portion. God is now
restoring all things, not dividing. God is preparing the "one
new man" by taking the Ruths and the Naomis and joining
those two into one—producing the double portion. Identify
yourself as coming from the same family and lineage as Israel
through the Jewish Messiah, Jesus (*Yeshua* in Hebrew), and

pray for their salvation; you will then begin to enter into the double portion.

Those who watch and pray for Jerusalem, helping her to rebuild her ruins spiritually as well as physically, will receive double portion glory.

> *Because I love Zion, I will not keep still. Because my heart yearns for Jerusalem, I cannot remain silent. I will not stop praying for her until her righteousness shines like the dawn, and her salvation blazes like a burning torch* (Isaiah 62:1 NLT).

> *O Jerusalem, I have posted watchmen on your walls; they will pray day and night, continually. Take no rest, all you who pray to the Lord. Give the Lord no rest until He completes His work, until He makes Jerusalem the pride of the earth* (Isaiah 62:6-7 NLT).

Chapter 10

ANCIENT SECRETS TO WORLDWIDE HARVEST

There are ancient keys that will unlock and accelerate worldwide harvest more than anything else on the planet; they are seldom used but are now being revealed once again. This revelation is the master key. Just as there are many keys that open up different rooms in a hotel (the guest rooms, gym, restaurant, and lobby, etc.), there is a master key that will open up multiple doors in Heaven's storehouse of mass harvest, blessing, and multiplication.

Paul, himself a descendant of the Hebrew people and the apostle most learned in the Hebrew Scriptures, was able to take that knowledge and revelation and bring it into the New Covenant. The results were unprecedented. Paul was a master harvester. He won more souls in large stadium-style meetings, planted more churches, discipled more people, and became the most-read author and apostle to the present day. He brought a holy revolution to both the church and the Roman Empire.

He moved in unusual signs, wonders, miracles, and resurrection power. Paul had the faith and ability to even present the gospel to the ruling powers of his day, converting the ruler of Cyprus, almost converting Governor Felix while still in chains, and never stopping until he got to Rome to speak to the head of the Roman Empire.

What was Paul's secret? What did he know then that most do not know today? How did he magnify his ministry many times over even after his death? How was he able to convert so many Jews and Gentiles alike and shake the foundations of the ruling empire of his day? Let's explore another mystery of the ancients.

> *For I speak to you Gentiles; inasmuch as I am an apostle to the Gentiles, I magnify my ministry* (Romans 11:13).

In the next verse we will learn a simple secret that will propel any person, ministry, or nation into limitless possibilities of great magnification as we dig into this profound yet often missed truth: *"I magnify my ministry, if by any means I may provoke to jealousy those who are my flesh and save some of them"* (Rom. 11:13-14).

Paul simply explains to Gentile believers in Rome the master key to the success of his life and ministry. His secret is that he would always go to the Jews first with the gospel, make them jealous for the Messiah, and try to save some of them. Why would this be the master key to world harvest then or today? You see, Paul was called by God to take the gospel to the Gentiles, which shocked the early Jewish church. His initial desire was to be called to the Jews, but God had other plans for Paul's main ministry. Paul had a key that would win more Gentiles than anything else. He knew the Hebrew writings that said, *"I will bless those who bless you [Israel], and I will curse him who curses you"* (Gen. 12:3).

Paul knew that if he would first bless Israel with salvation, his ministry to the Gentiles would be magnified a thousand times greater than if he did not. When a ministry reaches out to the ancient people of Israel, it causes a supernatural tidal wave of blessing and harvest in the Gentile world. When one Jew gets saved, it accelerates worldwide salvations, open doors, and harvest. But why?

TWO-FOLD GREAT COMMISSION

The Bible talks about going into all the world, preaching the gospel, and then the end will come (see Matt. 24:14). So most people think that if we target every Gentile nation with the gospel, including the last unreached nations, that this will trigger the return of the Lord, and then somehow Israel will be saved at the end. The problem is that this is only half the truth. It is the slow route that Christianity has been taking. Even if you reach every nation right now, if Israel is not reached, the Lord cannot return. Why is that? The reason is in this next verse: *"See! Your house is left to you desolate; and assuredly, I say to you, you [Israel] shall not see Me until the time comes when you say, 'Blessed is he who comes in the name of the Lord!'"* (Luke 13:35).

Here Jesus is talking about Israel and the people of Jerusalem right after He prophesies to the Jewish people in Jerusalem. The Messiah will not return to the earth or Israel again until there is a remnant of Jewish people asking Him to come back. Once there are a certain number of Jewish Israelis who know

Jesus their Messiah personally and call Him back, His return is very close. That being said, if every Jew that you help to get jealous or saved brings Jesus closer to returning, then get this. If it speeds up His return, it speeds even faster the worldwide harvest of souls among Gentiles. It also accelerates your ministry to the Gentile world and speeds up the time clock. What would take you ten years to see with regard to harvest, salvations, and promises from God could suddenly start occurring in weeks and months. I can only count on one hand how many people are actually implementing this strategy, but the few who do are seeing phenomenal results, and their ministries are exploding with harvest and ridiculous favor.

Some examples of this are Mahesh Chavda Ministries' "Watch of the Lord" that prays every week, has recruited literally hundreds of hours of prayer worldwide for the nations, and always prays for Israel in every aspect each week. Mahesh Chavda was a disciple of Derek Prince and also ministered with him. Derek Prince, himself a great healing evangelist and teacher, taught the principles of blessing Israel and praying for Israel, and even resided in Israel until his death, ministering to the people there with healings and miracles.

Sid Roth, host of *It's Supernatural*, attributes his entire success in reaching millions worldwide with salvation and healing to his principle of reaching the Jew first, opening up some of the greatest doors of the gospel on both secular and Christian television. He has explained that supernatural provision has always occurred, and he has not used fundraising on television to support the ministry—which is amazing— not to mention the many miracles, healings, and salvations that occur. (Other great ministries like Lester Sumrall, Ruth

Ward Heflin, and even Benny Hinn give or have given a great portion of their time and ministry to ministering in Israel and have publicly stated the need to support Israel in her time of need.)

The Bible clearly says that the gospel is to the Jew first (see Rom. 1:16). Here, God was not saying that the gospel will come to the Jew first, and that later in history it will come mainly to the Gentiles until His return. No way. The gospel is always for Israel and, in fact, to be shared with the Jew first. This Scripture is talking about God's preferred method of world evangelism then and now.

This is not to say that Israel or the Jews are more special, for God loves all nations, but this is about strategy. He chose to bring the Messiah out of the Jewish people. He now chooses to use the Gentiles and born-again Jewish believers to bring them back in. We owe a debt to the Jewish people and Israel for bringing us the Messiah, and to the 12 Jewish apostles who risked all to bring the gospel to the Gentiles—which would include most of you reading this book.

Here are Jesus's last words before He left the earth, outlining the strategy one last time:

> But you shall receive power when the Holy Spirit
> has come upon you; and you shall be witnesses to
> Me in Jerusalem, and in all Judea and Samaria,
> and to the end of the earth (Acts 1:8).

From Jerusalem to the end of the earth. Start to pray for Jerusalem, Israel, and Jewish people to be saved so that it can speed up the harvest of souls in your city and nation.

THE GENTILE KEY

In Romans 10:1-2, Paul says, *"My heart's desire and prayer to God for Israel is that they may be saved. For I bear them witness that they have a zeal for God, but not according to knowledge."* He goes on to explain that he knows they are trying to achieve righteousness by their own works, and he would know because he was a Pharisee of Pharisees. But he says that God wouldn't let him reach Israel as his main and only call.

Right before this, he says, *"I tell you the truth in Christ, I am not lying, my conscience also bearing me witness in the Holy Spirit, that I have great sorrow and continual grief in my heart. For I could wish that I myself were accursed from Christ for my brethren, my countrymen according to the flesh"* (Rom. 9:1-3). Such was the depth of his love for Israel and the Jewish people that he was willing to go to hell if that would save the Jewish people.

Paul weeps before God for the Jewish people as Jesus did, wanting to reach his own people, but God confirms to him that his calling is to the Gentiles. God unlocks the mystery, showing Paul that as the Gentiles come in, the Jews will be provoked to jealousy and will then come in. Now Paul gets excited. A light bulb of revelation goes off. He sees that the strategy to get the Jews saved is to get many Gentiles saved so that the Jews become jealous for their Messiah. So Paul is thinking, *"OK, God, if that's how it is going to work, if the Gentiles need to get saved so that they in turn start making Israel jealous to be saved, then let me at them, at the entire Gentile world. I am even going for the leader of the Gentile world in Rome."* Paul now goes full throttle to the Gentile world, moves to Rome, and probably hopes to reach as many as possible in his lifetime, so he can speed up the salvation of Jews in Israel.

One of your first calls as a believer in the Jewish Messiah is to make Israel jealous once again by your life in Jesus. This will take much more than just words: *"For Jews request a sign..."* (1 Cor. 1:22).

Every believer in Jesus has a calling to the Jewish people in Israel and around the world, to make them jealous by your salvation, love, healing, signs and wonders, family, blessings, etc. Have you been making any Jewish people jealous lately? Reaching Israel accelerates salvation worldwide among Gentiles, and reaching those Gentiles with salvation who will love Israel also speeds up Israel's revival. As you go to the nations to bring in the harvest, do it with a goal that these Gentiles will get Israel saved.

Paul went to the other extreme as he started to reach the other nations with a passion, evangelizing, planting churches, and ministering to the other ends of the world. To magnify his ministry to the world, he always reached the Jew first.

THE CREATOR OF HEAVEN AND EARTH

Humankind had the knowledge of the One True God of Heaven from the beginning since Adam. As the nations were dispersed because of rebellion at the Tower of Babel, they carried with them the accounts of creation, the Garden of Eden, Noah and the universal flood, as well as God's requirements for forgiveness and reconciliation and the blood covenant. Moses wrote down the creation story; however, Moses, like his contemporaries, already had knowledge of the beginnings of the world, which was passed down through oral tradition. This same knowledge was carried into the rest of the world as the nations were dispersed from Babel. That would explain why many unevangelized, even primitive, societies have in their tribal traditions a concept of a Creator God who reigns supreme over all. Many of these tribes and nations had an almost identical account of Genesis, Noah and the flood, Babel, and the knowledge that blood sacrifice was required, just like God had told Adam and Eve. That being so, then all nations had a general knowledge of the Creator God and also had the same chance to reconcile with God when that provision of reconciliation was made in the person of Jesus Christ.

Consider the Chinese. From the very beginnings of their civilization, this knowledge of the power of God is expressed in the following song found in *The Collected Statutes of the Ming Dynasty*:

> Of old in the beginning, there was the great chaos, without form and dark. The five planets had not begun to revolve, nor the two lights to shine. In the midst of it there existed neither form nor sound. You O spiritual Sovereign, came forth in Your sovereignty, and first did separate the impure from the pure. You made heaven. You made earth. You made man. All things became alive with reproducing power.

This should not surprise us that other nations and cultures had an understanding of the One God of Heaven and earth, as Paul writes: *"For since the creation of the world His invisible attributes, His eternal power and divine nature, have been clearly seen, being understood through what has been made, so that they are without excuse"* (Rom. 1:20 NASB).

If one can understand this ancient mystery that all tribes and nations at one time had an understanding and believed in the same One True God of Heaven, the Creator, then God can release a supernatural model to bring in the Gentile nations to the gospel of Jesus. Because this has not been understood, the gospel has been limited among many tribes.

The Korean church is a good modern example of using this ancient wisdom to reach an entire nation, and it's also an example of what not to do out of ignorance and western pride in our way of presenting the gospel.

The Catholics arrived in Korea first and preached in the name of their "foreign" (it was foreign to the Koreans) God. They received little response. In 1884, Protestant missionaries, after researching the name of the Korean Supreme Being and Creator, began using the name of the benevolent Creator God, Hananim, in their preaching. They taught that Jesus Christ was the Son of Hananim and that Hananim had sent Jesus to bring the Koreans into a new relationship with Himself. Thousands of Koreans listened in awe that these missionaries knew so much about their God, Hananim.[38] The news began to shake Korea. This is one of the reasons a great revival started in Korea with long-lasting fruit, as Korea is now sending out more missionaries than any nation in the world, not to mention that the three largest churches in the world are in Korea.

Many of us in the western Christian world may need to humble ourselves and ask God to forgive us of cultural prejudices, which have hurt many native people and thus damaged the work of the gospel in native lands. Especially here in North America, with all the gospel that goes out from our continent, some of the least evangelized people groups to this day are the

Native Americans living in America because of the way the gospel was first presented.

The Navajos, the Hawaiians, and many other tribes had a belief in and great respect for the Creator as the Supreme God over all. The Navajo Indians would never mention their One True God to the "white man," as it had been decided long ago among their elders. The reason being was because they revered the One True God as so sacred and precious to them that they could not bear to have the white man belittle, laugh at, ridicule, or call their God the devil simply because it was not the same pronunciation that the white man had for their God in their language.[39]

The Chinese name for the One True God was Shang Ti. When the missionaries first came, they had the same low response as in Korea until they realized that the same Creator God in Genesis was what they called Shang Ti. Once that was understood, the gospel began to take off like wildfire, touching even those in the royal court because of the message that Jesus was the Son of the Creator God whom the Chinese called Shang Ti.[40]

The Chinese already understood man's need for a blood sacrifice thousands of years ago. Their emperors used unblemished bulls for their sacrifices to Shang Ti, because these animals were more costly than all others, and because imperial sacrifices were made to cover the sins of the entire nation, as was the case with Israel. Officials and ordinary people could use lesser sacrificial animals because these people were atoning only for their own individual offenses. The ancient Chinese clearly understood that righteousness is imputed through an acceptable sacrifice. No wonder when the gospel was finally explained as the Son of the Creator Shang Ti, who was the final sacrifice to atone for man's sins and bring him into relationship with God once again, they understood it, as they were already prepared from the beginning to hear about the greatest unblemished sacrifice of God's Son.[41]

God is the Creator of all nations, tongues, and peoples and is spoken of in each language. Instead of belittling the One True God in another language, we should instead introduce Jesus to them as the Son of their Creator God. God did create them from the beginning and never left them without a witness and sent His Son to die for them out of great love for all nations.

When Christianity came to Hawaii, there was confusion because they already had a Supreme Being. Malia, who spoke Hawaiian as her first language, was mentored by the most respected Hawaiian authority of modern times, Mary Kawena Pukui. She explained that Hawaiians believed in the Creator and One True God called 'Io in Hawaiian.

In an interview in the Iolani newspaper, Malia related that her ancestors said:

> Let us go to this church and listen to their minister. If it is good and they are right in their teaching about their powerful God of the universe, then we will keep that same God. The reason is that we have a God like theirs. If they are exaggerating that their God is better than our God, they are wrong. We Hawaiians have had a powerful all-knowing God from the beginning until today.[42]

Her elders accepted Jehovah but never told the missionaries about 'Io because they knew that their God would be ridiculed and called the devil by the missionaries. However, she would hear her Kupuna (elders) say while praying, "Jehovah, you are 'Io."

It is also amazing that there are references to 'Io in the literature of different Maori tribes well before the Old Testament was introduced to New Zealand. 'Io was so much like the Hebrew God Yahweh that at first researchers assumed that it evolved with Christian teaching. They later discovered it was in their beliefs long before the white man or the Scriptures arrived.[43]

The Polynesians had an almost identical account of Abraham, Isaac and his sons, Joseph, Moses, Jonah, and even the idea of cities of refuge as recorded in the Bible. This is a testimony that God has already prepared humankind with the knowledge of the One True God to hear about His Son who can save them and reconnect them with the God the Creator once again.

Chapter 11

THE ISHMAEL-MUSLIM CONNECTION

Romans 11:25 says that *"blindness in part has happened to Israel until the fullness of the Gentiles has come in."*

According to Faisal Malick, (a former Muslim who is now a believer with a worldwide ministry and television host on the Miracle Channel in Canada) in his book *Here Comes Ishmael*, says that nearly 42 percent of the world's Gentile population is Muslim.[44] That means that as we start to reach the last remnant of the Gentile world, the Muslims, more Jews in Israel and worldwide will be saved as the veil gets lifted. As you accept the call to take the gospel to the Muslims, you will also be part of lifting the veil off the Jews; and as you bless the Jews and reach them with salvation, it will trigger greater harvests among the Gentiles. We are noticing as we go to the Muslim world that we begin to see a greater harvest and openness in Israel each time. And every time we go to Israel, great opportunities to bring the gospel to the Muslim nations open up.

The Muslim harvest will also trigger a harvest of souls in many other nations. Probably some of the largest untouched harvest fields of the world today are the Arab and Muslim nations. (Not all Muslims are Arabs; many Muslims are Persians, as in Iran, and many are also Asian, as in Indonesia and Malaysia.) Romans 11:11 says, *"To provoke them to jealousy, salvation has come to the Gentiles."* Who better to provoke Israel to jealousy than the descendants of Ishmael?

The greater your love for Israel and the Jewish people, the greater will be your love for the descendants of Ishmael. It's not one or the other. They're family. When you take the gospel to the Jew first, you actually get a greater love for the Arabs. People who are anti-Semitic usually don't like either of them. I saw a bumper sticker once that said, "I'm not racist, I hate everybody." It's all interconnected. As the Jews receive the gospel, the Muslim world opens up to the gospel and vice-versa.

> *I will provoke you to jealousy by those who are not a nation, I will move you to anger by a foolish nation* (Romans 10:19).

Another translation of "those who are not a nation" is those who are "no people." This means a people of no covenant with God, strangers to the promises of God made to Israel through Isaac. After Ishmael was cast out, God even referred to Isaac as Abraham's only son (see Gen. 22:2; Heb. 11:17). So to Israel, Ishmael is no longer a part of the picture. Ishmael, who mocked Isaac from the beginning, would certainly be the most likely not only to provoke jealousy but also to provoke anger as they come into covenant with God. In Israel's eyes, Ishmael and the Muslims are still mocking them in war, violence, threats, and terrorism.

The Muslims are the last of the Gentiles that Israel would see as deserving of salvation. The salvation of the Muslim people who were cast out of inheritance into the wilderness will greatly provoke Israel to a holy jealousy and anger and will lead to a new passion to seek the Messiah of Israel, Jesus.

The barometer is increasing worldwide. In the last few years I have observed something happening; people are more open now than ever before in coming to the Messiah in both Israel and the Muslim world. As we do more in Israel, God is simultaneously opening the Muslim and Arab world to us. It is not either/or; it's the whole family of Abraham, starting with Isaac, and including Ishmael and the rest of the world. God blessed both Isaac and Ishmael in different ways. There are also ancient portals of revival and masses of untouched harvest fields in the Arab and Muslim world waiting to be reaped. As we pray for and reach Israel, God will unlock the ancient gates to the Arabs and Ishmaelites. The ancient gate to Ishmael is through first touching and recognizing their brother Isaac.

Remember, the order that triggers favor and harvest involves bringing the gospel "to the Jew first." That is where supernatural favor will open to you in a great way. We just experienced this in Dubai, Qatar, and Kuwait, where we not only reached the local people but even prayed with one of the government leaders who also got healed. In large, packed-out meetings, we had standing room only and touched Egyptians, Iranians, and people from all over the Middle East—as well as India and Sri Lanka. We have also done major outreaches in Indonesia and Malaysia as well, which are some of the largest Muslim nations in the world.

The Jews are going to get jealous at the Gentiles getting saved. When the Arabs get saved and start to love the Jews back, it is going to astonish the Israeli Jews especially. When the believers in Lebanon, for example, are not only saved but full of love for their Jewish Israeli brothers, celebrating biblical feasts, and praying for Israel's salvation, it is going to dumbfound the Jewish people. They'll start wondering, "How can this be happening?" Remember, the festivals are not just Jewish festivals; they are God's festivals for all of God's people. These Arab believers who no longer hate Israel and who also have God's glory, love, and power will provoke the Jews to jealousy; they will wonder how in the world their enemy got the God of Israel on their side. It's really hard to have the God of Israel on your side if you hate or dislike Israel. God even named Himself "the God of Israel" (see Isa. 45:3).

God is also calling Jewish believers (and all believers) to take a risk and bring the gospel to the Arab and Muslim world. I can see this happening prophetically, and it has already started. The explosion of the glory of God is waiting to be unleashed as Jewish believers dare to take it to the Arab world. Many more Jewish believers are called to bring the gospel not only to their own people, but to the Gentile world, especially to the sons of Ishmael. Paul knew the ancient pattern and worked it both ways, going to the Jew first and reaching multitudes of Gentiles, and reaching Gentiles with zeal to draw the Jews to their Messiah.

THE WEALTH OF THE GENTILES

Through a single seed, through Isaac, God chose to bring the Messiah. Since the time of Adam, God prophesied that the seed coming from Abraham, Isaac, and Jacob would crush the head of the serpent and bless the whole world. Though the covenant was made only through Isaac, Ishmael did receive a blessing as well:

And as for Ishmael, I have heard you. Behold, I have blessed him, and will make him fruitful, and will multiply him exceedingly. He shall beget twelve princes, and I will make him a great nation (Genesis 17:20).

Even though Ishmael lost the blessing of Abraham and any inheritance from his father at the time, God still invoked a blessing on him separately that still is there today, not just in population and land mass, but in wealth.

There is a vast accumulation of wealth stored up in the Muslim world today. A publication of Cornell University reports that, according to professor of geological sciences, Muawia Barazangi, "two-thirds of the world's proven recoverable oil reserves exist in the Persian Gulf."[45] The Middle East supplies more than double the oil of the rest of the world combined. Wealth has been stored up for thousands of years in the Muslim world and is still being laid up; they are also investing it worldwide in land and real estate. The Ishmaelites were businessmen from the beginning who traded all over the known world, carrying vast caravans of goods as a way of life.

I will give you the treasures of darkness, and hidden riches of secret places, that you may know that I, the Lord, who call you by your name, am the God of Israel (Isaiah 45:3).

We know that in the last days there will be a transfer of wealth from the kingdom of darkness into the Kingdom of light for the spreading of God's Kingdom, as prophets have been prophesying this for decades now (see Isa. 60:5,11). The vast billions of dollars of hidden wealth the Bible speaks about are also hidden in the Muslim world. As Cyrus was told about "treasures of darkness and hidden riches of secret places," he was blessed to be a tool in blessing Israel even though God tells him, *"I have named you, though you have not known Me"* (Isa. 45:3-4). God clearly tells him the purpose for blessing him as Isaiah 45 continues to reveal why God is giving such treasure: *"For Jacob My servant's sake, and Israel My elect, I have even called you by your name"* (Isa. 45:4).

Amazingly, Cyrus was from Persia—modern-day Iran— which is now one of the key Muslim nations in the world, controlling most of the world's oil as its second largest producer in the world. God used and blessed Cyrus—who was from a nation normally at war with Israel—to be a blessing to Israel. Not only did Cyrus free the Jews from 70 years in captivity in Iran to return to Israel—which few heathen kings willingly did—but he commanded the Babylonians who lived near Jewish survivors to contribute toward their expenses by supplying them with silver and gold, supplies for the journey, and livestock, as well as a freewill offering for the Temple of God in Jerusalem. He also returned all the stolen items from the Temple when Nebuchadnezzar had captured Jerusalem (see Ezra 1:1-8).

Why has God hidden the vast amount of untapped wealth in the Muslim world and the descendants of Israel? Why did God promise Abraham blessing over Ishmael even though Isaac received the spiritual blessing? Is it any wonder that Ishmael's descendants have tapped into such wealth via oil in the last days, since Abraham still asked for a blessing over his other son?

This is where things get interesting. God has blessed the Muslim world with the greatest wealth, and I believe their wealth will be released to expand the Kingdom of God on the earth as He did in the days of old. This is according to Isaiah 60, which talks about the flocks of Kedar and other descendants of Ishmael, as well as past references in the Bible of God using the wealth of Israel's enemies to bless them—as with Esther in Babylon, Cyrus, and many other biblical patterns—so that they come to know Jesus.

God had purposely promised to Abraham to bless Ishmael from the beginning, keeping this treasure safe in the dark, hidden places within the Muslim world, storing it up to come into the Kingdom of God for the last days, when the oil and the wealth it produces would be a commodity. I believe God is going to use Ishmael, the Muslim nations, to play a big role in financing the end-time harvest. As we begin to evangelize and pray for the Muslim world's salvation, the release of billions and even trillions of dollars in the greatest transfer of wealth will be triggered, similar to the transfer of the wealth of Egypt to God's people in the Exodus.

Once Muslims receive Jesus, they will as passionately support the gospel with their wealth as they once did Islam, for which many were willing to die. Their passion and zeal for God will be hard to match.

The Bible talks about the wealth of the Gentile nations coming in, and particularly mentions in Isaiah 60:6, *"The multitude of camels [that] shall cover your land, the dromedaries of Midian and Ephath."* Verse 7 states, *"All the flocks of Kedar shall be gathered together to you."* Camels are surely a sign of the Muslim nations, while Kedar was the second son of Ishmael (see Gen. 25:13), and, according to tradition, an ancestor of Mohammed, the prophet of Islam.

Not only will Muslims support the gospel, but, according to Isaiah 60, they will also use this money to bless Israel. Isaiah 60:3 says, *"Gentiles shall come to your light, and kings to the brightness of your rising."* This prophecy speaks to the people of Israel, the descendants of Isaac, proclaiming that one day the Ishmaelites will come back to bless the God of Israel in Jerusalem.

Isaiah 60:13 declares to Israel that *"the glory of Lebanon shall come to you, the cypress, the pine, and the box tree together."* The word *glory* also means wealth in this passage. Imagine the wealth of Lebanese Arab believers blessing Israel financially and spiritually toward revival. God will cause a holy reconciliation between Isaac and Ishmael through the Messiah, Jesus. The passage goes on to explain that those who afflicted Israel the most throughout the generations will come back and make peace with gifts.

> *Also the sons of those who afflicted you shall come bowing to you, and all those who despised you shall fall prostrate at the soles of your feet; and they shall call you the City of the Lord, Zion of the Holy One of Israel. Whereas you have been forsaken and hated, so that no one went through you, I will make you an eternal excellence, a joy of many generations. You shall drink the milk of the Gentiles, and milk the breast of kings; you shall know that I, the Lord, am your Savior and your Redeemer, the Mighty One of Jacob* (Isaiah 60:14-16).

Again, this Scripture describes the descendants of Ishmael who will once again return to Israel with gifts. Even now, this will start to happen as those from the Middle East will long to bless Israel toward salvation with their gifts and testimony. This will culminate when the Messiah returns to Jerusalem, and the nations such as Egypt will come up every year to Jerusalem to celebrate the Messiah together (see Zech. 14:16).

On our last tour to Israel, we visited with a group from the oil-rich Gulf States of the Arab world. We had a hard time getting some of them visas to get through because of their Muslim names. God made a way at the last moment when the minister of the interior finally stamped their visas after a heated exchange with the tour company who promised they were now believers in Jesus and loved Israel. When the Israeli soldiers saw them come across the bridge through Jordan, they welcomed them with smiles and chocolate, congratulating them for their courage to come to Israel, since they risked persecution if their nation ever found out.

The Arab believers also feared being rejected by the Israelis, but instead they said they felt such love and curious friendship even by the Israeli soldiers. And to top it off, this occurred during the Feast of Tabernacles just recently, a prophetic foreshadowing of what is to come. Shortly afterward, we had the most amazing miracle meetings in their country and even met with a government official in a neighboring country.

PURPOSE FOR THIS WEALTH

And you shall remember the Lord your God, for it is He who gives you power to get wealth, that He may establish His covenant which He swore to your fathers, as it is this day (Deuteronomy 8:18).

The purpose of the great wealth transfer is to establish His covenant. It is the covenant that God made with Abraham to bless all the families of the earth through his Seed, Jesus. That means that wealth is first and foremost a means for spreading the gospel. God will allow the sons of Ishmael to be part of establishing God's covenant in the earth as they use this wealth to spread the gospel worldwide.

We know that the earth and its fullness is the Lord's, including the oil wells. God knew very well that in the last days oil would be the main commodity, and He is reserving Ishmael to establish His covenant in the end times with Isaac. Ishmael will trade the earthly oil for the oil of the Spirit of Heaven, and this oil will quench the thirst that has plagued him in the wilderness.

Chapter 12

THE RISE AND FALL
OF NATIONS

There are ancient mysteries that will cause a nation to rise or to fall based on the wisdom and knowledge of the ancients imbedded in the Word of God. America, for example, has seen significant blessing and has risen as one of the most blessed nations on the earth by following these time-tested, ancient blessings. But will it last? It really depends on us.

Historically, every world empire that had the most Jews within its borders or the most direct influence with the Jewish people were also among the most powerful nations on the earth, and those same nations fell based on what they did to the Jewish people.

We know that Egypt at one time subjected most of Israel to slavery (see Exod. 1:7-14). As a result of the blessing that rested on the sons of Isaac, Egypt was the most wealthy and powerful nation in the world. The moment they went against God concerning His people, the same nation experienced the worst of devastations, never to rise again to world prominence. The same went for the Babylonians, modern-day Iraq, and other empires that dealt harshly with God's people, even though God allowed this suffering due to Israel's failings (see Isa. 50:17-19).

The Roman Empire had control and rule over all of Israel. Once they destroyed Jerusalem and the glory lifted, however, Rome began a fast descent and finally lost its world domination.

In more recent history, Spain reigned as the world's most powerful empire for 500 years during the time when most of the Jews in the known world lived there. Anti-Semitism began to rise in the fourteenth century, but the demise of the Spanish Empire can be traced to the day (March 31, 1492) Ferdinand and Isabella of Spain issued the Edict of Expulsion.[46]

The British Empire was once a mighty empire with colonies all over the world and the largest naval fleet; its military power dominated large parts of the world, including Africa, India, parts of Asia and Hong Kong, and Middle Eastern nations. Britain also exerted control over Palestine from 1919 through the time of World War II. The Balfour Declaration of 1917 "led the Jewish community in Britain and America into believing that Great Britain would support the creation of a Jewish state in the Middle East."[47] Subsequently, many Jews (and Palestinian Arabs) felt they had been betrayed, when, at the end of World War I, Britain "was given Palestine to govern by a League of Nations mandate."[48] The end of Britain's supremacy began, in my view, when the Exodus, a ship of Jewish refugees en route to Palestine in 1947, finally made it within sight of her shores. The British, who were still governing Palestine, sent them back to British-controlled camps in postwar Germany.[49] The result was that Britain ultimately lost control of Palestine, and then every other colony in the world, leaving them today with scattered overseas territories and a homeland which is troubled from within by extreme Muslim groups and recent terrorist attacks.

Now the U.S., with its 5 million Jewish Americans, the largest Jewish population in the world, has been thrust onto the scene as the world's greatest military and economic power. America was the first to recognize Israel as a nation and has helped the nation both economically and as a military ally. Also, many evangelical Christians have prayed for and supported Israel. It seems that we are now at a crossroads.

As I said before, nations with the largest Jewish population at any given time have almost always become world powers—partly due to the blessing of hosting the descendants of Isaac. Also, America has now taken England's role in becoming a dominant nation with direct influence on the nation of Israel. If we misuse this same source of blessing, it can be our downfall. That is why we need to pray for our nation's leaders to have wisdom in their dealings with the nation of Israel, as it will have direct consequences on the stability and survival of America.

> For behold, in those days and at that time, when I bring back the captives of Judah and Jerusalem, I will also gather all nations, and bring them down to the Valley of Jehoshaphat; and I will enter into judgment with them there on account of My people, My heritage Israel, whom they have scattered among the nations; they have also divided up My land (Joel 3:1-2).

The verse above is talking about a time after the Holy Spirit falls on all flesh and during a time when the Jewish people return to Israel. It is at a time when the nations are together talking about dividing up the land of Israel. Joel 3 pertains specifically to our time when these events—the return of the Jews to Israel and the division of the land—have lined up. Joel 3:1 says, *"In those days and at that time."* What days, what time? The time is now—when the Jews are brought back from the nations to which they were scattered, when a worldwide outpouring of the Holy Spirit occurs, when talk of dividing up the land of Israel becomes prominent.

After the U.S. recently urged Israel to give away the Gaza Strip, almost immediate disaster struck America. I remember it well, seeing on Israeli television on August 15, 2005, as soldiers were forced to evacuate their own Jewish brothers and sisters from their land. News reports came in of soldiers who refused and were punished for it; others went into depression for having to do something totally against their conscience.[50]

As I watched the footage, the Lord told me to pray for the U.S., as something devastating was about to happen, but prayer could lessen the effects. We left Florida shortly after the Gaza Strip evacuations, driving right through New Orleans. When we passed through New Orleans, the Lord led us all to pray for the people of the city but not to stay the night. By the time we arrived in Arizona, we saw footage of Hurricane Katrina destroying the city. I believe this was a direct result of our nation pressuring Israel to give up Gaza, which biblically is promised to Israel. Many Palestinians now say they were much happier when the Israelis were in Gaza, as there was more freedom and economic stability for them, and Gaza itself is increasingly overrun by terrorists, violence, and great danger. I have noticed that the Israeli Arabs living as Israeli citizens with full rights of health care, voting, owning businesses, etc., are much happier than Palestinian Arabs who do not want to be under Israel's rule. You never hear of Israeli Arabs choosing to move over to the Palestinian side. They are living in the shared blessing of the land of Israel, living in more peace and stability than the neighboring Arab nations.

The Gaza area was a productive agricultural center which is now lost. The economic impact of Hurricane Katrina on New Orleans and the nation was significant—primarily affecting oil supply and exports.[51] To this day there are still Jewish families from Gaza living in hotels, tents, and temporary housing, trying to start all over again; the same is true for many displaced families who lost everything in New Orleans. Both lost homes. Jewish graves had to be dug up and relocated. In New Orleans, the flooding opened many graves, and bodies were floating around as well. The Bible is very clear about the fact that quick retribution will follow any nation that divides His land.

Another time we were in Israel, and on the news I saw our president announce that he would be the first president to divide Israel and give the Palestinians their own nation. As soon as I heard this, my spirit was grieved, and a great burden fell upon me. I knew that the president was not trying to do this maliciously, but that he probably really believed this was humanly the best solution. That is the problem; we have to see God's point of view concerning His land. Following this decision, the space shuttle Columbia launched into space. It was a historic flight—the first time an Israeli astronaut went into space with Americans. On reentry, the space shuttle Columbia divided and exploded over Texas. I remember headlines reading, "Space Shuttle Divides over Palestine, Texas." Palestine entered the news in February 2003, as one of the East Texas towns that received much of the Columbia disaster debris.[52] I believe it was a direct result of our nation's intention and was only a warning. Obviously, it was not heeded as we experienced Hurricane Katrina after the Gaza pullout incident that the U.S. also encouraged and pressured.

During that time, I also had a clear dream while in Jerusalem. I dreamed that I met the U.S. president at a U.S. embassy as I was renewing my passport overseas. I told him that we were praying and had even fasted for him to be elected. Then I looked into his eyes and said with tears streaming down my face, "But please do not divide Jerusalem." That was back in 2003, before Gaza was given up, so I could not understand why my dream was about the division of Jerusalem. Now we see clearly that the division of Jerusalem is what is being negotiated even as you read this. If this occurs, the U.S. or any other nation that brokers this deal, even with the best of intentions, will experience the most devastating consequences.

I recently spoke to a well-known prophet, asking his opinion about what would happen if America actually was able to pressure Israel to give up half or part of Jerusalem to the Muslim Palestinian government. His answer was that he believed that a massive earthquake along the Madrid fault line would split America in half from Chicago to Mississippi—the Mississippi River would run backward, and land travel from east to west would become nearly impossible. But it could be much worse than this.

I was in Trinidad the day after sending a mass email to pray for the Annapolis Peace Conference, releasing a word that I sensed earthquakes could be the result if we did not pray. I asked God for a confirmation that what I was saying was right. The next day we went to Trinidad to minister. Within less than five minutes of walking off the plane toward customs, a 7.0 earthquake shook the airport, the island, and many surrounding islands, including Jamaica. I also received an email which said that Arkansas, which lies on the Madrid fault line, also had a 2.0 earthquake.

Let us not test God in this area, but pray for mercy and a change in our dealings with the nation of Israel. There is also a window of grace to pray for a reversal of judgment and a major revival and move of God. It could be that we will have shakings and revival simultaneously, reaping the prayers of revival and the consequences of sin. We are praying that many will turn things around toward massive harvest and revival in America, which is also upon us in this hour.

PAST RESULTS OF DIVIDING ISRAEL

Remove not the ancient landmark which your fathers have set up (Proverbs 22:28 AMP).

On August 23, 1992, Round 6 of the Madrid Peace Conference began in Washington D.C.[53] The key Israeli-Palestinian issue involved negotiations to set up interim self-rule for Palestinians.[54] The acting U.S. representative and Secretary of State Lawrence Eagleburger, in an interview with the New York Times about the Peace Conference, said the talks were resuming "in the context of an Israeli Government that is prepared to be far more forthcoming."[55] He predicted that the issue of the Palestinian self-rule in the Israeli-occupied territories would be the focus of the discussion. Within 24 hours, on August 24, 1992, Hurricane Andrew smashed into southern Florida.

Hurricane Andrew was the worst natural disaster to hit America up to that time. It left 180,000 in Florida homeless, and another 25,000 in Louisiana. The damage was estimated to be as high as $26.5 billion. This was an awesome Category 5 hurricane with top winds recorded at 175 miles per hour; however, the wind-measuring device was destroyed before the eye hit. The winds may actually have been as high as 200 mph. This storm was described by the National Hurricane Center as a 25- to 30-mile wide tornado.[56]

Hurricane Andrew struck the opening day of the conference. The next day there was a story in the news about President Bush's ratings collapsing in the polls. In one day three major events occurred—the Madrid Peace Process met for the first time on American soil, the destruction caused by Hurricane Andrew, and the collapse of the Presidency of George H. W. Bush. Bill Clinton suddenly began leading in the polls by a substantial margin.[57] Just a year before, President Bush had a tremendous approval rating and was expected to be reelected to a second term. After the Gulf War, President Bush's ratings were as high as 89 percent, according to the Gallup poll. Shortly before Round 6 of the Madrid Peace Conference in Washington D.C., the Gallup poll recorded what would be the lowest approval rating of Bush's presidency—29 percent; President Bush's hopes of reelection were fading.[58] The convergence of the Madrid Peace Conference, Hurricane Andrew, and Bush's presidential woes in the larger context of U.S. support of Israel are certainly worth noting.

Amazingly, President George W. Bush has also had very low approval ratings; the connection between his attempt to implement the division of Israel and Jerusalem, and the downturn in those ratings must be examined. History repeats itself time and time again as God's ancient principles of not touching the land or people of Israel apply for us today.

JULY 1997

The entire world through the United Nations came against Israel in March, April, and July 1997.[59] On July 2, the world economy had already started to unravel. Jerusalem and the land of Israel had taken center stage in world politics. The U.N. wanted the disputed land in Israel given away and Jerusalem divided. As the nations were planning to punish Israel economically, the world economy was shaken. Many nations in Asia were reduced to poverty. The economic meltdown started in Asia, then spread to Russia and later Brazil. None of these nations voted to support Israel in the United Nations. As the nations of the world were coming against Israel economically, their own economies were being destroyed.

> *And it shall happen in that day that I will make Jerusalem a very heavy stone for all peoples; all who would heave it away will surely be cut in pieces, though all nations of the earth are gathered against it* (Zechariah 12:3).

JANUARY 1998

On January 20, 1998, Israeli Prime Minister Benjamin Netanyahu met with President Clinton.[60] The meeting was to discuss the stalled peace plan and for Israel to give away some of its land. In the lead-up to the meeting, Netanyahu was under tremendous political pressure. Clinton was pressuring Israel to give away the land for the peace process. In Israel, there was pressure on Netanyahu not to give away land. The pressure was so great that politicians in Israel threatened to pull down his government if he gave away the land. Netanyahu met with Clinton and was coldly received. Clinton and Secretary of State Albright refused to have lunch with him. Shortly after the meeting ended, a sex scandal involving Clinton became headline news. Clinton became totally involved in the scandal and couldn't devote any time to Israel. He met with Arafat the next day, but there was no effort to pressure Israel to give away land. Netanyahu came to the meeting with the possibility that his government might fall. How ironic that right after the initial meeting, it was President Clinton's administration that was in trouble. The president was humiliated and faced legal action and possible impeachment. The very day Clinton was pressuring Israel to give land away was the day he was humiliated in a sex scandal. Netanyahu returned to Israel as a "conquering hero" because he did not give away any land.

SEPTEMBER 1998

On September 24, 1998, President Clinton announced he was going to meet with Yasser Arafat and Israel's Prime Minister Benjamin Netanyahu when they both came to New York City to address the United Nations.[61] The purpose of the meetings was to discuss the stalled peace plan in which Israel was to give away an additional 13 percent of its land. On this same day, the headlines of the national newspapers said that Hurricane Georges was gaining strength heading toward the Gulf of Mexico. The headlines of USA Today stated, "Georges gaining strength, Killer storm zeros in on Key West."

On September 28, Arafat addressed the United Nations and talked about an independent Palestinian state by May 1999. Arafat was given a rousing and sustained ovation as he addressed the General Assembly. As Arafat was speaking, Hurricane Georges was smashing the Gulf Coast, causing $1 billion in damage.

During the time Arafat was in the United States for the purpose of dividing Israel, Hurricane Georges was pounding the Gulf Coast. Arafat left America, and the hurricane then dissipated. God judges the nations that divide His land, according to Joel 3, and blesses those that bless God's ancient covenant people.

"I will bless those who bless you, and I will curse him who curses you" (Gen. 12:3). God sets before us two paths, blessings or curses. Let's choose the blessing of God and align our lives with God's purposes for His covenant people, land, and nation.

NOVEMBER 1998

The stock market recovered from the crash of July-September and went on to record highs.[62] During the week of November 23, the market reached its all-time high. On November 30, Arafat came to Washington D.C. and met with President Clinton. He came to raise money for his Palestinian state, and he also said that in May 1999 he was going to declare a Palestinian state with Jerusalem as the capital.

A total of 42 other nations were represented at this meeting in Washington. All the nations together agreed to give Arafat $3 billion in aid. President Clinton promised that the United States would give $400 million and the European nations pledged $1.7 billion.

As President Clinton was meeting with Arafat, the stock market was crashing, and it fell for a total of 216 points that day. The economic pundits could not explain why the stock market crashed other than for profit taking. The radio news reports for November 30 had the Mideast meetings and the stock market crash as stories following each other. The meeting and the crash were headline stories the next day in some of the nation's newspapers. The articles were even touching each other on the front page.

On December 1, the European stock markets crashed in the third worst crash in European history. How ironic that as the nations of the world met to promise $3 billion in aid for a Palestinian state, their own stock markets crashed.

Historically, and even in our modern age, as the nations of the world continue to pressure Israel to give up covenant land in Israel and Jerusalem, their economies start to crumble or rise depending on their relations with Israel. America is now the leader in dealing with Israel, having the power and influence to force Israel into giving up land in exchange for America's "protection" and financing. We need to pray for mercy over our nation and the nations of the world so that neither we, nor the nations we pray for, will have any part in dividing up Israel.

SEPTEMBER 11, 2001

On September 11, the greatest attack ever on American soil occurred.[63] The hijacking of four planes and the attack on the World Trade Center in New York City and the Pentagon in Washington D.C. left upward of 3,500 dead. These suicide attacks by Muslim terrorists caused approximately $40 billion in damage and stunned the country. On this day, America came under the attack of terrorism on an unimaginable scale. More Americans died on September 11 than during the attack on Pearl Harbor or the D-Day invasion.

The attack on the World Trade Center came without warning and was aimed right at the financial heart of the United States. The largest stock brokerage firms in the world were in the World Trade Center, along with many of the international banks. The effect of this attack on the stock market was devastating. It may have been the catalyst for a worldwide economic depression. What could the U.S. have done to open the door to such a disaster?

On August 9, 2001, a suicide terrorist killed 19 Jews and wounded over 100 people in a Jerusalem pizzeria. Later that day, President Bush made a speech condemning the terrorist attack. After condemning the attack, the president then demanded that Israel abide by the Madrid Peace Process, the Mitchell Plan, and United Nations Resolutions 242 and 338. An excerpt of the President's speech follows:

> The United States remains committed to implementation, in all its elements, of the Mitchell Committee Report, which provides a path to return to peace negotiations based on United Nations Security Council Resolutions 242, 338, and the Madrid Conference. To get to Mitchell, the parties need to resume effective security cooperation and work together to stop terrorism and violence.[64]

These U.N. resolutions called for Israel to go back to the borders prior to the Six-Day War of 1967, requiring Israel to give up East Jerusalem, the Golan Heights, and all settlements on the West Bank. The president was totally ignoring the covenant Israel has with God. He was telling Israel to go back to borders that were indefensible, thus putting Israel in a very dangerous position. He then ended the speech by telling Israel to negotiate with the very people who had just committed a horrible terrorist attack.

On October 2, 2001, major news sources reported that at the time of the attack on 9/11, the U.S. government was in the process of recognizing a Palestinian state. Just prior to September 11, the Bush administration had formulated a policy of recognizing a Palestinian state with East Jerusalem as its capital.[65] The secretary of state, on September 13, was going to notify the Saudi Arabian ambassador of this plan, and it was going to be announced by the secretary of state at the U.N. General Assembly on September 23. The attack on September 11 derailed this plan. At the very time the U.S. was going to force Israel into coexistence with terrorists who were dedicated to the destruction of the Jewish nation, the U.S. came under attack by the same terrorists.

Since September 2000, Israel had been the subject of continued terrorist attacks, and the terrorists have killed hundreds of Jews. Israel was engaged in a low-grade war being waged by the Palestinians. In the face of the terrorism and war, President Bush wanted Israel to negotiate with the Palestinians and give away covenant land, including East Jerusalem.

Exactly 32 days later, the Muslim terrorists struck America. America had now come under the same type of terror that the Israelis were under. America was heading into war against Muslim terrorists just like the war Israel was engaged in. Israel was fighting for its very existence, and now America was in the same battle for existence.

As America has forced Israel to give up sections of the covenant land, the identical pressure has come upon America.

Below are some of the parallels between what happened in Israel and America since September 2000. These parallels are:

- At the same time the Israeli government was destabilized in late 2000, so was America's.

- Almost a year to the day that the intense terrorism began against Israel, America was attacked by the same type of terrorists.

- Jerusalem, the capital of Israel, was under terrorist attack, and Washington D.C. was also under attack by terrorists.

- Israel was in a low-grade war with Muslims; America also entered into a low-grade war with Muslims.

- Americans came under the same fear that the Israelis live under.

- Israel's economy suffered because of the terrorism. The American economy fell under the same pressure.

- The tourist industry collapsed in Israel because of the terrorism. The tourism industry in America—not to mention New York itself, one of the most visited cities in America—began to collapse right after the terrorist attacks of September 11, and many feared to travel by air after the attacks. Also, major airlines began filing for bankruptcy and many employees were laid off.

Losses were estimated at $39.7 billion across the industry.[66]

Whenever America, our beloved country, has mistakenly pressured Israel to give up land for "peace," we have always suffered as a result, especially on September 11, 2001.

MERCY TRIUMPHS OVER JUDGMENT

Recently I was invited to speak at the U.N. to the workers and officials. During this time, I prophesied that the U.N. would not succeed that day in dividing Jerusalem. This was on Wednesday, November 14, 2007. Soon after, we discovered that the U.N., on the floor directly above, was holding a last-minute meeting without notifying the press; they were trying to rush a vote to divide Jerusalem with the Israeli ambassador to the U.N. present. Later, we realized that key people like the president did not show up, and the vote could not go through. We believe we were sent by God to intercept the plans of the enemy; we were able to delay God's judgment as we asked for mercy and declared that the enemy's plans would not succeed that day.

I believe that we as God's people have the authority to delay and even alter many planned attacks and premature judgments and to declare God's favor and revival instead. We should definitely be aware of the dangers we face as a nation for our actions and then boldly pray and declare the opposite while repenting and pleading for mercy.

There seem to be two camps. One camp wants to prophesy destruction as Jonah did over Nineveh, almost hoping it will happen just so they will be proven accurate. This is wrong. But there is the other extreme, which is often a reaction to the doom and gloom. This other camp totally avoids even warning God's people of possible judgment and only focuses on the love and grace of God without sounding a prophetic alarm to avert disaster. This also is wrong. We need to be balanced in the middle ground, clearly knowing the Word of God, trumpeting those warnings as watchmen on the wall, believing God for a mighty revival and harvest of souls, and basking in God's protection, love, and grace. We need to understand God as the lover of our souls, but also as the judge of the nations. We need to believe that mercy triumphs over judgment if we will simply cry out for mercy in these times—as well as explain to God's people and the heads of nations what the Word of the Lord says concerning standing with Israel. This is also a major key to following the ancient paths as we align ourselves with God's plan for His ancient people, land, and nation.

BLESSING HIS BRETHREN

Assuredly, I say to you, inasmuch as you did it to one of the least of these My brethren, you did it to Me (Matthew 25:40).

In this passage, Jesus was speaking of His Jewish brethren. Many interpret this as an injunction to help the poor: *"As you have done it to the least of these—the poor—you have done it unto Me."* Of course we should help the poor, but this verse is taking about the Jewish people and Israel. In Luke 7:4-5, we read of Jewish elders who ask Jesus to bless a Roman centurion for his generosity to the Jewish people. Jesus then healed the centurion's servant. Jesus never said that helping Israel does not merit a blessing; on the contrary, when he heard this, he blessed that Roman for blessing the Jewish people.

As you begin to tap into this wisdom and ancient portal to the glory of God by blessing, standing with, and praying for revival and harvest in Israel, a new wave of the favor, glory, and blessing of God will begin to invade your life.

ENDNOTES

1. Werner Keller, *The Bible as History* (New York, NY: Bantam, 1983), 209.

2. Ibid., 210.

3. John Bright, *A History of Israel* (Westminster: John Knox Press, 2000).

4. Ibid., 95, 154.

5. Ibid., 81–92.

6. Keller, 199–202.

7. Barry Fell, *Bronze Age America* (New York, NY: Little, Brown and Co., 1982), 261.

8. Leonard and McGlone, "An Epigraphic Hoax on Trial in New Mexico," *Epigraphic Society Occasional Publications* 17 (1988), 206.

9. Ibid., 130–131.

10. Bloom and Polansky, "Translations of the Decalogue Tablet from Ohio," *Epigraphic Society Occasional Publications* 17 (1988), 206–219.

11. Ibid., 96.

12. Ibid., 186.

13. Ibid., 168.

14. Keller, 202–203.

15. Alan Taylor, *American Colonies: The Settlement of North America* (London: Penguin Books Ltd., 2003), 33.

16. Chuck Missler, "Mysteries Behind Our History: Was Columbus Jewish?" Koinonia House Online. Retrieved from http:// www.khouse.org/articles/1996/109.

17. FreeRepublic.com, "Missouri Cherokee Tribes Proclaim Jewish Heritage," FreeRepublic.com. Retrieved from http://www.freerepublic.com/focus/f-news/848921/posts.

18. Hope-of-Israel.org, "Who Really Discovered America?" Hope of Israel Ministries. Retrieved from www.hope-of -Israel.org./hebinusa.htm.

19. Barry Fell, *America B.C.* (New York, NY: Pocket, 1989), 310.

20. Daniel I. Kikawa, *Perpetuated in Righteousness* (Keaau, HI: Aloha Ke Akua Publishing, 1994), 136–137.

21. David Herzog, *Desperate for New Wine* (Renew, 1998).

22. *Encyclopedia Britannica* 11th ed., 8, 828–829. Also the definition of Easter in *Webster's* dictionary clearly shows its pagan origin.

23. Fred Mobley, "Is Easter Biblical," found at http://www .reflecthisglory.org/study/easter.htm (accessed September 12, 2013).

24. Eusebius, *Vita Constantine*, Lib. III, 18–20.

25. Philip Schaff and Henry Wace, eds., *Nicene and Post-Nicene Fathers: Second Series, Vol. XIV* (Grand Rapids,

MI: William B. Eerdmans Publishing Company, 1974), 54–55.

26. George Buttrick and Keith Crim, *The Interpreter's Dictionary of the Bible*, 3 (Nashville, TN: Abingdon Press, 1976), 933–934.

27. *Collier's Encyclopedia*, 3 (New York, NY: Macmillan Educational Company, 1986), 13.

28. Edward Davies, *The Mythology and Rites of the British Druids* (Whitefish, MT: Kessinger Publishing, LLC, 2003), 210.

29. James Bonwick, *Egyptian Belief and Modern Thought* (Indian Hills, CO: Falcon's Wing Press, 1956), 211–212.

30. Eusebius, *Ecclesiastical History* (Peabody, MA: Hendrickson Publishers, 1998), 86–88.

31. Kevin Trudeau, *Natural Cures "They" Don't Want You to Know About* (Brooklyn, NY: Alliance Publishing, 2004), 170.

32. "Heresy." *The Catholic Encyclopedia* (New York: Robert Appleton Company, 1910).

33. E. Gibbon, *The Decline and Fall of the Roman Empire*, 3 (New York, NY: Everyman's Library, 2004), 76.

34. Jacobo Di Voragine, *The Golden Legend: Selections* (New York, NY: Penguin Classics, 1999).

35. Roberts Liardon, *God's Generals* (New Kensington, PA: Whitaker House, 2003).

36. "Aliyah." Wikipedia, The Free Encyclopedia. Retrieved from www.en.wikipedia.org/wiki/Aliyah.

37. Jerusalem Post.

38. Don Richardson, *Eternity in their Hearts* (Ventura, CA: Regal Books, 1984), 62–71.

39. Kikawa, 60.

40. Chan Kei Thong, *Faith of our Fathers* (China Publishing Group, Orient Publishing Centre, 2005).

41. Ibid., 69.

42. Kikawa, 59.

43. Peter H. Buck, *Vikings of the Pacific* (Beverly Hills, CA: Phoenix Books, 1960), 274.

44. Faisal Malick, *Here Comes Ishmael: The Kairos Moment for the Muslim People* (Bellville, Ontario: Essence Publishing, 2005).

45. Anne Ju, "Amid debate..." Cornell University Chronicle Online. Retrieved from http://www.news.cornell.edu/stories/Jan07/barazangi.oil .aj.html.

46. "History of the Jews in Spain." Wikipedia, The Free Encyclopedia. Retrieved from http://en.wikipedia.org/wiki/ History_of_the_Jews_in _Spain.

47. Chris Trueman, "The Balfour Declaration of 1917." History Learning Site. Retrieved from http://www .historylearningsite.co.uk/ balfour_declaration_of_1917 .htm.

48. Ibid.

49. Gregory Katz, "Documents Show British Dilemma." ABC News. Retrieved from http://abcnews.go.com/International/WireStory?id=4784854&page=1.

50. Laura King, "To Obey Orders or Obey God." *Los Angeles Times*, August 8, 2005; http://articles.latimes.com/2005/aug/08/world/fg-dissent8 (accessed July 14, 2008).

51. "Economic Effects of Hurricane Katrina." Wikipedia, The Free Encyclopedia. Retrieved from http://en.wikipedia.org/wiki/Economic_effects_of_Hurricane_Katrina.

52. "Palestine." Wikipedia, The Free Encyclopedia. Retrieved from http://en.wikipedia.org/wiki/Palestine.

53. John McTernan and Bill Koenig, *Israel: the Blessing or the Curse* (Oklahoma City, OK: Hearthstone Publishing Ltd., 2001), 63–64.

54. "Madrid Conference of 1991." Wikipedia, The Free Encyclopedia. Retrieved from http://en.wikipedia .org/ wiki/ Madrid_Conference of 1991.

55. McTernan and Koenig, 63.

56. "Hurricane Andrew Is Termed Third Worst in This Century." *New York Times*, September 18, 1992; http://query.nytimes.com/gst/fullpage.html?res =9E0CE2DB1E3DF93BA2575AC0A964958260&sec =&spon= (accessed August 3, 2008).

57. McTernan and Koenig, 64.

58. Frank Newport, "Bush's 69%." Gallup. Retrieved from http://www.gallup.com/poll/106741/Bushs-69-Job -Disapproval-Rating-Highest-Gallup-History.aspx. This website contains information on the ratings of both Presidents George H. W. Bush and George W. Bush.

59. McTernan and Koenig, 72–73.

60. Ibid., 73–74.

61. Ibid., 75.

62. Ibid., 77–78.

63. Ibid., 97–100.

64. Ibid., 98.

65. Daniel Mandel, "Try, Try, Try Again: Bush's Peace Plans." *The Middle East Quarterly*. Retrieved from http://www.meforum.org/ article/642#_ftn38.

66. Jimmy Nesbitt, "Kentucky Tourism Still Affected." *Knight Ridder/Tribune Business News*, January 14, 2004. http://www.allbusiness.com/government/government-bodies-offices/10255212-1.html

ABOUT DR. DAVID HERZOG

DR. DAVID HERZOG is the founder of David Herzog Ministries based in beautiful Sedona, Arizona. David is a dynamic speaker and bestselling author who appears often on TV and Radio. He moves in creative miracles, healing, and signs and wonders worldwide. He also equips believers to operate in fresh revelation and the glory and power of God. David and his wife, Stephanie, have seen multitudes saved and equipped in practically every continent and in over 50 countries. David's passion is to live in the glory of God and to bring the Gospel to as many souls as possible in every nation of the world.